ROYAL NAVY HOME FLEET 1939–41

The last line of defence at Scapa Flow

Angus Konstam
Illustrated by Jim Laurier

OSPREY PUBLISHING
Bloomsbury Publishing Plc
Kemp House, Chawley Park, Cumnor Hill, Oxford OX2 9PH, UK
29 Earlsfort Terrace, Dublin 2, Ireland
1385 Broadway, 5th Floor, New York, NY 10018, USA
E-mail: info@ospreypublishing.com
www.ospreypublishing.com

OSPREY is a trademark of Osprey Publishing Ltd

First published in Great Britain in 2024

A catalogue record for this book is available from the British Library.

ISBN: PB 9781472861481; eBook 9781472861450; ePDF 9781472861467; XML 9781472861474

24 25 26 27 28   10 9 8 7 6 5 4 3 2 1

Maps by bounford.com
Diagrams by Adam Tooby
Index by Mark Swift
Typeset by PDQ
Printed and bound in India by Replika Press Private Ltd.

Note
All 'miles' referred to in this text are nautical miles.

Photographs
All photos in this book are courtesy of the Stratford Archive.

Front Cover: Art by Jim Laurier, © Osprey Publishing
Osprey Publishing supports the Woodland Trust, the UK's leading woodland conservation charity.

To find out more about our authors and books visit www.ospreypublishing.com. Here you will find
extracts, author interviews, details of forthcoming events and the option to sign up for our newsletter.

CONTENTS

THE FLEET'S PURPOSE

When war broke out in September 1939, the Royal Navy was divided into several fleets or 'stations'. The largest of these, and the Royal Navy's main striking force, was the Home Fleet. Containing the bulk of the Royal Navy's capital ships, cruisers and fleet destroyers, this powerful fleet would inevitably be Britain's first line of defence against the German Kriegsmarine, much as the British Grand Fleet had been during the previous war. As in 1914–18, the fleet's main objective was to maintain a naval blockade of Germany by bottling up its German counterpart inside the North Sea – sealing off the English Channel to enemy vessels and U-boats, and establishing a patrol line along the northern side of the North Sea. However, the fleet had other key duties too, the most important being the countering of any invasion attempt on the British coast. The fleet's arena of responsibility was also larger, as the Home Fleet's commander was responsible for operations not just in the North Sea but also in the North Atlantic.

In World War I the Grand Fleet stood ready to counter any German sortie into the North Sea, and to bring the High Seas Fleet to battle in a decisive engagement. That need for readiness still applied in 1939, although the possibility of a traditional fleet engagement was now minimal. What had changed during the inter-war period was the development of air power, the effectiveness of submarines and the size of the rival battlefleets.

In 1939, while German air power was effective, it was poorly placed to support naval operations in the North Sea, let alone farther afield in the Atlantic. By contrast British airfields were ideally sited to support the blockade, and to conduct search or attack missions if required. Similarly, in 1939, while U-boats were more effective than their predecessors of the last war, they still lacked the numbers to make a significant impact on the naval war. However, the sinking of the battleship *Royal Oak* in Scapa Flow in mid-October was one of the most spectacular of several U-boat attacks on major units of the Home Fleet during this period.

In 1939, the German surface fleet had two battleships available, and several powerful cruisers. These were to be used as surface raiders, and at the outbreak of war, two of these armoured cruisers (*Deutschland* and *Graf Spee*) were already in the North Atlantic. The prevention of a sortie by German surface raiders into the North Atlantic became a major task for the Home Fleet until the sinking of *Bismarck* in 1941.

From the outbreak of war until the late spring of 1940, the Home Fleet was able to seal off access to the Atlantic by patrolling the waters between Orkney and the Norwegian coast. This was relatively easy to maintain thanks to their proximity to the fleet's base in Scapa Flow and Coastal Command's airfields. Even then, a second patrol line existed running northwards along the line from Orkney to Shetland, then on to the Faeroe Islands, and then Iceland. A further patrol in the Denmark Strait between Iceland and Greenland ensured that all possible routes to the Atlantic were blocked. However, this system was not infallible, as weather, the availability of ships and the poor visibility in long winter nights all hampered the effectiveness of the system.

The German invasion of Denmark and Norway in April 1940 completely altered the strategic landscape. It forced the Home Fleet to abandon its Northern Patrol line between Orkney and Norway. It was now untenable due to the establishment of Luftwaffe bases in Norway. This meant the stopgap patrol line running from Greenland to the Scottish mainland became the new front line in the naval campaign. This, of course, meant that the maintenance of a constant naval blockade became much harder due to the distances involved. The fall of France that summer gave the Germans direct access to the Atlantic. If German surface raiders succeeded in breaking out into the Atlantic, they no longer needed to return home the way they had come. Instead they could make for Brest or St. Nazaire, and use these French ports as bases for further operations. This placed an even greater strain on the Home Fleet. The only consolation for the British Admiralty was that, unlike bases in Germany, these French ports lay within relatively easy reach of British bombers.

The full might of the Home Fleet, arrayed around the white-hulled *Empress of Australia* in May 1939 before the liner carried the King and Queen to Canada for a state visit. In the foreground is the fleet flagship, the battleship *Nelson*, flying the flag of Admiral Forbes. Astern of *Nelson* is the destroyer *Somali*, followed by the fleet carrier *Ark Royal*.

Inevitably, the nature of the Home Fleet's primary mission changed during the first two years of the war. The fall of France raised the spectre of a German invasion of Britain. The Home Fleet already had a mission to protect the British Isles from attack, and attention now focused on the English Channel. While direct naval command there was already apportioned to other regional commands, it was now expected that the Home Fleet would stand in readiness to oppose any cross-channel invasion. This led to the drafting of a new set of plans, and to the fleet itself remaining ready to counter any such attack.

This was linked to another problem. By 1940, the Battle of the Atlantic was well under way, and the U-boat threat was increasing. Therefore, as the demand for convoy escorts increased, it was inevitable that the Home Fleet was called upon to provide fleet destroyers for escort tasks. The supply of 50 obsolete Lend Lease destroyers from the United States eased the situation somewhat, but the need for fleet destroyers remained. The invasion threat brought a temporary end to this, as the bulk of these fleet destroyers were retained in home waters for anti-invasion duties. However, the Admiralty continued to divert Home Fleet warships for other duties, such as service in the Mediterranean, or for special operations farther afield.

The other drain on the Home Fleet's strength came from German commerce raiding. From the start of the war, warships had to be withdrawn from the fleet to hunt down raiders. The fleet's older battleships were also frequently deployed as powerful convoy escorts, as were a number of cruisers and fleet destroyers. This all added to the strains on the Home Fleet's commander, who was often left with barely enough warships to cover the routes into the Atlantic, or to counter any powerful German sortie. Nevertheless, as Admiral Tovey's reaction to the *Bismarck* sortie showed, in time of crisis the Admiralty was able to divert other assets to reinforce the Home Fleet, which gave Tovey the ships he needed to pursue and ultimately to destroy the *Bismarck*.

This operation marked a sea change in the mission of the Home Fleet and brought an end to German surface raiding operations in the Atlantic. Although the need to block German access to the Atlantic remained, the Home Fleet could now be deployed in other operations, in home waters in other theatres. Then, in June 1941, Hitler's armies invaded the Soviet Union. This led to a requirement to send supplies to the beleaguered Soviets, and a sea route was opened up between Britain and the northern Russian ports of Archangel and Murmansk. The need to protect these convoys, and the resulting redeployment of much of the German surface fleet to Norway, ushered in a new era for the Home Fleet. From that point on, until the end of the war, its primary mission would be to support the Arctic Convoys, but this is a subject for another book.

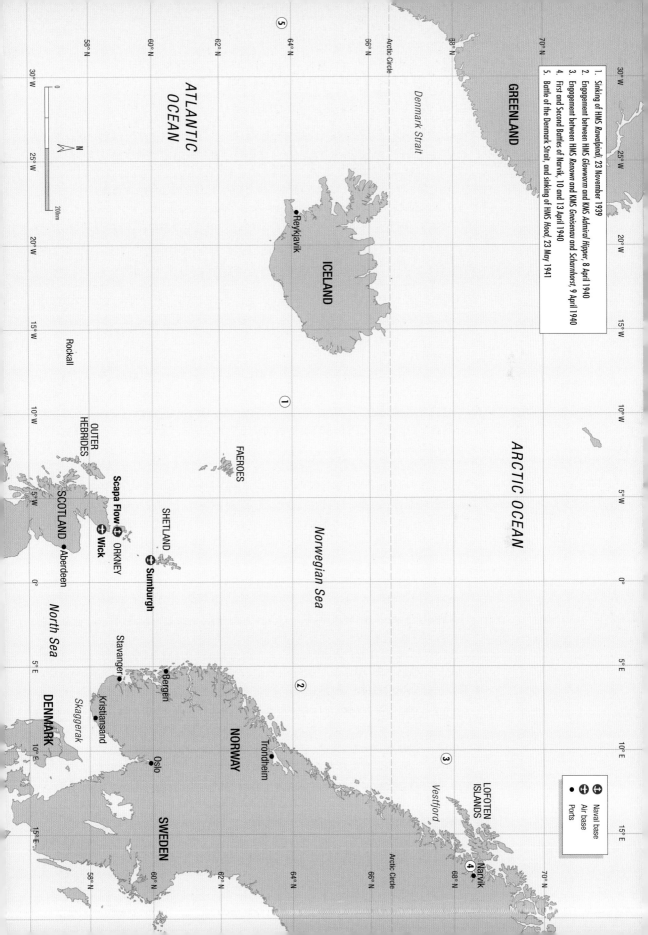

ATLANTIC OCEAN

ARCTIC OCEAN

GREENLAND

Denmark Strait

ICELAND

Reykjavik

⑤

Arctic Circle

70° N
68°
66°
64°
62°
60°
58° N

30° W
25° W
20° W
15° W
10° W
5° W
0°
5° E
10° E
15° E

1. Sinking of HMS Rawalpindi, 23 November 1939
2. Engagement between HMS Glowworm and KMS Admiral Hipper, 8 April 1940
3. Engagement between HMS Renown and KMS Gneisenau and Scharnhorst, 9 April 1940
4. First and Second Battles of Narvik, 10 and 13 April 1940
5. Battle of the Denmark Strait, and sinking of HMS Hood, 23 May 1941

Rockall

①

FAEROES

Norwegian Sea

OUTER
HEBRIDES

Scapa Flow ✛ ORKNEY
SCOTLAND ● Wick
SHETLAND
✛ Sumburgh
● Aberdeen

North Sea

Stavanger
● Bergen

Kristiansand
Skaggerak

● Oslo

NORWAY

Trondheim

②

Vestfjord

③

LOFOTEN
ISLANDS
Narvik ④

Arctic Circle

SWEDEN

DENMARK

✛ Naval base
✛ Air base
● Ports

N

0   200nm
(scale bar)

FLEET FIGHTING POWER

THE SHIPS

When the war began, the Home Fleet was a powerful, well-balanced force. It was made up of a mixture of modern warships and elderly ones, although as Britain's primary line of defence, the fleet had the first priority in terms of modern warships. It was therefore strong enough to challenge anything the Kriegsmarine could throw against it. In September 1939, the fleet consisted of two aircraft carriers, five battleships, three battlecruisers, a heavy cruiser, six light cruisers and 17 fleet destroyers. These were supported by a number of auxiliary vessels such as minesweepers, drifters and supply vessels. The aircraft carriers were commanded directly by the Commander-in-Chief of the Home Fleet, Admiral Sir Charles Forbes. The other major warships were grouped into three squadrons, one of battleships, one of battlecruisers and a third of the fleet's assorted cruisers. The destroyers were similarly grouped into three flotillas. Forbes could also draw on other cruisers and destroyers deployed in Rosyth on the Firth of Forth.

On paper this was a far more potent force than the two battleships, three armoured cruisers and five heavy and light cruisers available to the Kriegsmarine. Nevertheless, the five battleships were all old and slow, and all of them apart from the two capital ships of the Nelson class had seen service during World War I. Only the fleet's three battlecruisers had the speed to catch the German battleships *Scharnhorst* and *Gneisenau*, and even then only *Hood*, flagship of the battlecruiser squadron, had the firepower and protection needed to take them on with any likelihood of success. The cruisers, however, were fast enough to establish a patrol line, and if contact was made, they would shadow the enemy and guide the capital ships of the Home Fleet until they brought their more modern German counterparts to battle.

Of course, this was a largely pre-war view of naval power, based around the firepower of the battleship. The likelihood of a Jutland-style fleet duel was

The battlecruiser *Hood*, arguably the most famous pre-war ship in the Royal Navy, pictured at anchor in Scapa Flow during 1940. Off the port bow are torpedo nets, designed to protect the main fleet anchorage, while barrage balloons can be seen behind the battlecruiser.

slim. Instead, the Home Fleet found itself involved in maintaining a naval blockade – first the Northern Patrol between Britain's Northern Isles and the Norwegian coast, and then, after the fall of Norway, running in an arc from the Northern Isles as far as Greenland, by way of Iceland and Greenland. This had three immediate effects on the fleet. First, as the distances involved were much greater, the blockade would require more warships to make it as effective as before. Secondly, if this blockade was to be maintained at all times, this placed a considerable physical strain on the ships and their crews. This could be alleviated only by rotating warships between spells of active patrol duty and periods of respite in Scapa Flow, or repair in British shipyards. This accordingly increased the number of ships needed to make the blockade effective.

Given the challenging weather conditions which could be expected for much of the year in Icelandic or Faeroes waters, destroyers and other lighter vessels were less well suited to blockade work than cruisers. Thus, a system evolved where an advance patrol line made up of auxiliary cruisers would provide early warning of any enemy attempt to break the blockade. Then a second line of light cruisers, equipped with radar, would present a more significant barrier. Ideally, behind them, more cruisers, including heavy cruisers, would be available to shadow any intruder, and harry it, while directing other larger units to the area, which could attack and sink the enemy. This last group usually meant the arrival of forces from the Home Fleet's battlecruiser squadron, which had the speed to react quickly to calls of support. As a final resort, the battle squadron itself would put to sea, led by the Home Fleet's commander-in-chief, and it would take up the task of bringing the enemy to battle.

In addition, to help these capital ships locate their target, the Home Fleet's admiral would ideally have one or more fleet carriers at his disposal. These served two purposes. First, they could help locate the enemy, and direct the

Fairey Swordfish torpedo bombers ranged on the after end of the flight deck of the fleet carrier *Victorious*, in May 1941, during the pursuit of the German battleship *Bismarck*. These semi-obsolete biplanes, crewed by raw airmen, would carry out a night attack on the German battleship in mid-Atlantic.

fleet's surface ships towards it. The carrier could also launch its own air strike against the enemy force, using torpedo-armed biplanes. While these might not sink their target, they could at least damage it, allowing the capital ships of the Home Fleet to overhaul the enemy force and engage it in a surface action. Air power was equally important in bolstering the blockade. This, for the most part, would be supplied by the Royal Air Force. During the Norwegian campaign of 1940, the shortcomings of this arrangement were exposed. So too were the difficulties encountered by the RAF in attacking enemy naval forces. Arguably the Fleet Air Arm was better suited to anti-shipping operations, as evidenced by their sinking of the German light cruiser *Königsberg* off Bergen in 1940.

The Home Fleet had a substantial force of submarines attached to it. For example, in June 1940 this consisted of 24 submarines, formed into four active submarine flotillas. Two of these were based in Rosyth, one in Dundee and one in Tyneside. Like all submarines in home waters, they were under the overall command of Vice Admiral, Submarines – Vice Admiral Max Horton who had his headquarters in Portsmouth – they were also placed at the disposal of the Home Fleet's commander-in-chief. For the most part these were used in a reconnaissance role. To this end they would patrol in the Skagerrak, and off the coast of southern Norway, to detect any German warship movements and forewarn the Home Fleet of any potential attempt to break the blockade. Before the invasion of Norway they would also form part of the Northern Patrol. They could, of course, attack any suitable targets they encountered. However, this was considered a bonus – their main job remained the gathering of intelligence.

Throughout this period the Home Fleet was in a state of near-constant flux. Warships were regularly redeployed elsewhere, or sent off from Scapa Flow to undergo refits or repairs. In some ways this was no bad thing, as it allowed the Admiralty to alter the size and composition of the Home Fleet, to reflect the duties the fleet was expected to perform.

HOME FLEET, SEPTEMBER 1939

Fleet carriers (2)	*Ark Royal* (Ark Royal class); *Furious* (Furious class)
Battleships (5)	*Nelson, Rodney* (both Nelson class); *Royal Oak, Royal Sovereign, Ramillies* (all Royal Sovereign class)
Battlecruisers (3)	*Hood* (Hood class); *Repulse, Renown* (Renown class)
Heavy cruisers (1)	*Norfolk*
Light cruisers (5)	*Aurora, Sheffield, Newcastle, Belfast, Edinburgh*
AA cruisers (1)	*Calcutta*
Seaplane carrier (1)	*Pegasus* (in Tyneside)
Destroyers (17)	8 Tribal class, 9 F class
7 minesweepers, 1 target ship, 2 target service destroyers, 14 Admiralty drifters	

By the end of the gruelling Norway campaign of April to June 1940, the structure of the fleet had changed, to better reflect the new reality of German air and naval bases in Norway, and more in France. It also included several ships which were undergoing repair after receiving damage off Norway.

HOME FLEET, JUNE 1940

Fleet carriers (2)	*Ark Royal* (Ark Royal class); *Furious* (Furious class)
Battleships (4)	*Nelson, Rodney* (both Nelson class); *Barham, Valiant* (both Queen Elizabeth class)
Battlecruisers (3)	*Hood* (Hood class); *Repulse, Renown* (Renown class)
Heavy cruisers (4)	*Devonshire, Norfolk, Suffolk, York*; (2 more, *Berwick* and *Sussex* were under repair)
Light cruisers (3)	*Birmingham, Southampton, Newcastle* (5 more, *Aurora, Galatea, Penelope, Edinburgh* and *Glasgow* were under repair)
AA cruisers (0)	*Cairo* was under repair
Destroyers (24)	8 Tribal class, 2 D class, 13 E/F class, 1 G/H/I class; (8 more, 4 Tribal, 1 E/F, 3 G/H/I classes were under repair)
Escort destroyers (2)	2 Hunt class
Sloops (2)	2 Black Swan class
19 minesweepers, 1 depot ship, 3 survey ships, 1 rescue ship, 20 Admiralty trawlers and drifters, plus assorted boom vessels, tugs and harbour vessels.	

HOOD AND *PRINCE OF WALES* DEPARTING SCAPA FLOW, 22 MAY 1941 (overleaf)

In the early afternoon of 21 May, *Bismarck* and *Prinz Eugen* were spotted by an RAF photo reconnaissance aircraft in Grimstadfjord south of Bergen. The Home Fleet's commander-in-chief Admiral Tovey ordered his deputy, Vice Admiral Holland to prepare for sea. Shortly after midnight, Holland's flagship HMS *Hood* slipped her moorings in Scapa Flow and put to sea, followed by the brand-new battleship HMS *Prince of Wales*. They shaped a course through Hoxa Sound into the Pentland Firth, where their escorting destroyers were already waiting for them. Once safely out into the North Atlantic, Holland would steam towards the southern coast of Iceland, where he could intercept the German ships when they tried to reach the Atlantic. This

illustration shows the battlecruiser *Hood*, followed close astern by *Prince of Wales*, as they make the transit through Hoxa Sound at around 0030hrs on 22 May. The viewpoint is the mouth of Widewall Bay, looking west from the anti-aircraft battery at Herston in South Ronaldsay, across the narrow channel to Stanger Head on the neighboring island of Flotta. To the right is Hoxa Head, where a powerful gun battery guarded this principal entrance into Scapa Flow. On Stanger Head, where a second battery was sited, a signalling lamp flashes a message to Holland's flagship, wishing him a successful voyage. It wasn't to be. Just over 53 hours later *Hood* would be sunk by *Bismarck*, with the loss of all but three of her crew.

Jim Lauries

The 14in guns of Admiral Tovey's fleet flagship, *King George V*. These were mounted in three turrets – two quadruple and one twin. Despite their relatively small calibre, once their teething problems were overcome these proved extremely effective.

The nature of the fleet changed again over the following year, as newly built warships entered service with the Home Fleet, and others were released for service elsewhere. For instance, the first of the Illustrious class of fleet carriers was commissioned in May 1940, and while *Illustrious* was earmarked for service with the Mediterranean Fleet, the next one, *Victorious*, which entered service in May 1941, was destined to reinforce the Home Fleet. *Victorious* was immediately thrust into action during the hunt for the *Bismarck*. By contrast it was intended that all of the new King George V class of battleships would be sent to Scapa Flow. The first of these, the *King George V*, joined the fleet in December 1940, and became the flagship of the Home Fleet's new commander, Admiral Tovey.

Although no more heavy cruisers would be built, a number of new Fiji-class light cruisers and Dido-class anti-aircraft cruisers would see service with the Home Fleet, although most would be sent to the Mediterranean. The Admiralty was more generous when it came to destroyers, and the fleet received quantities of war-built destroyers of the J/K/N, L/M and O/P classes. There were, of course, never really enough cruisers to make the blockade completely impenetrable. However, these reinforcements, together with improved fleet base facilities at Scapa Flow, allowed the fleet commander-in-chief to fulfil his objectives. In essence, this meant having just enough cruisers to patrol the approaches to the Atlantic, and a powerful-enough main force of capital ships to hunt down any German raiders which managed to penetrate the blockade.

From the start of the war, both the Home Fleet's commander and the Admiralty were faced with the problem of their older capital ships. The battleships of the Royal Sovereign class were too slow to be of much use in northern waters, as they would take much too long to steam from Scapa Flow to their blocking positions in the event of an attempted German breakout. Fortunately the arrival of *King George V* and sister ship *Prince of Wales* allowed the Admiralty to reclassify these old battleships as secondary ones and redeploy them elsewhere. A handful saw service in the Mediterranean, and some would even make it to the Far East. The same was true of *Nelson* and *Rodney*. By 1941, these ageing battleships were deemed too slow for fleet operations, and so were relegated to a secondary role.

For much of 1940–41 however, most were used as heavy convoy escorts, to deter the larger German raiders from attacking their charges. Fortunately, they encountered German battleships only once, and on that occasion *Scharnhorst* and *Gneisenau* broke contact with the battleship *Ramillies* rather than risk suffering damage in a gunnery duel. Like other capital ship escorts they could be called upon to join the Home Fleet if the occasion demanded. For example, during the hunt for the *Bismarck* in May 1941 *Rodney* was taken away from convoy escort duty and sent to join Admiral Tovey's main battle fleet. *Rodney* may have been slow, but the battleship still carried a main battery of nine 16in guns. On 29 May, these guns, and those of Tovey's flagship *King George V*, were able to engage *Bismarck* and play their part in the battleship's destruction. It was fortunate for Tovey that *Rodney* was on hand to play a part in the action.

Despite all these changes, one thing remained constant throughout the first two years of the war. The Home Fleet remained a powerful, well-balanced naval force, and its ships were arguably the best available to the Royal Navy during this period. For example, from mid-1940 on, when the British Mediterranean Fleet was plunged into a hard-fought naval struggle with Italy's Regia Marina, the Admiralty still kept its most powerful assets in home waters; for the most part the battleships *Nelson* and *Rodney* remained in Scapa Flow, as did *Hood* and the majority of the Navy's fleet carriers. This in itself was a tacit recognition of the challenges facing the Home Fleet in its struggle against the Kriegsmarine. Only a large, powerful and well-balanced fleet would be up to the task of effectively containing its German foes.

The Fairey Swordfish was a reconnaissance aircraft as well as a torpedo bomber, although, if needed, the aircraft could also mount conventional bombs. A biplane, the structure was outdated even on entering service in 1936, but the aircraft was reliable, and remained in use with the Fleet Air Arm throughout the war. It was an 18in aerial torpedo like this that crippled the *Bismarck*.

TECHNOLOGY

While the general strategic situation facing the Home Fleet was similar to that of the Grand Fleet, naval technology had moved on considerably in the intervening decades. The most significant development was aviation. Largely undeveloped in 1914, by 1939 the commander of the Home Fleet could rely on aircraft to support the operations of his forces. First of all, maritime reconnaissance aircraft of RAF photo reconnaissance were available to range out across the North Sea, Norwegian or Arctic Seas, or even the North Atlantic. These could be used to locate any enemy ships at sea, which would allow the fleet commander the information he needed to intercept these enemy ships.

This is exactly what happened on the afternoon of 21 May 1941, when an RAF photo reconnaissance Spitfire spotted the German battleship *Bismarck* and the heavy cruiser *Prinz Eugen* anchored in a fjord near Bergen. Five days later, after *Bismarck* had evaded pursuit and was alone on the Atlantic, an RAF Coastal Command Catalina flying boat operating from Northern Ireland sighted the battleship to the south-west of Ireland. This allowed Admiral Tovey, Commander-in-Chief of the Home Fleet, to direct his ships in pursuit of the German battleship. Air power, too, played a major part in *Bismarck*'s eventual destruction.

Another great technological advance was the development of the aircraft carrier. By 1939 the Home Fleet possessed two, with embarked squadrons of both fighter and torpedo bombers. The Swordfish torpedo bomber doubled as a reconnaissance aircraft, and could be used to locate the enemy to a range of approximately 200 miles from the carrier. Fitted with an aerial torpedo, the Swordfish could then attack the enemy – a relatively new offensive option, but one that could be effective. It was a torpedo-armed Swordfish that crippled *Bismarck* late on 26 May, allowing Tovey's battleships to bring her to battle.

As in World War I, reconnaissance by light warships was still a feature of naval warfare, so when searching for an enemy, cruisers still proved the most versatile for naval reconnaissance. Like the frigates of Nelson's Navy, they were the Home

The battleship *Rodney*, sister ship of *Nelson*. This shows *Rodney*'s unwieldy appearance, with the main armament concentrated forward in three triple turrets. Equally distinctive was *Rodney*'s citadel forward superstructure, sited two-thirds of the way down the hull.

Fleet's 'eyes and ears'. This time, however, they were faster and better-armed than their World War I predecessors, and by 1939 a few of them were fitted with Radio Direction Finding (RDF) sets. By 1943, the American term 'radar' had been adopted. In Britain this new technology had been developed during the late 1930s, when Sir Robert Watson-Watt developed it in partnership with the Royal Navy's Signals School. By 1938, a primitive RDF set was fitted to the battleship *Rodney* and the light cruiser *Sheffield*. At the same time, similar technologies were being developed in both Germany and the United States, but at this stage of the war British RDF systems were superior to these others.

At first, priority was given to the RAF's need for a chain of land-based radar stations to protect the country from enemy air attacks. This proved its worth in 1940, during the Battle of Britain. The first naval set, Type 79Y, was an air warning radar, and at least in theory it could detect approaching aircraft at a range of up to 60 miles. A variant, Type 279 was then developed, which also had a modest surface search capability. Eventually, three types of radar were available – air warning, surface search and fire control. Naturally there was a fair degree of interplay between them – for instance range, bearing and altitude information on approaching aircraft could be passed to a fire control system serving a warship's anti-aircraft guns.

There were technical differences between these systems. For instance, metric search radars had a relatively broad beam, like a floodlight, while decametric gunnery radars had narrow beams, which were better suited to ranging fire. Eventually centimetric fire control radars were developed which had the narrowest beam of them all, ideal for detecting and targeting individual ships and aircraft. Initially the Navy's priority was the fitting of air warning radar sets into their ships. In 1940, as the threat of invasion was at its height, there was a major push to fit these sets in destroyers. These Type 286M air warning sets were crude, and had fixed aerials, which covered a 180° arc ahead of the ship. It could give a good indication of range, but none of bearing. By the end of the year, only 34 destroyers were fitted with the set – roughly a quarter of the Royal Navy's operational strength. Fourteen of these served in the Home Fleet.

These early sets had a very limited effectiveness. For example, the Type 79Y air warning set carried in *Rodney* was unable to detect low-flying aircraft, although it was found it could detect surface warships at a range of around 10–12 miles. The emphasis was on 'could', as these sets were found to have an effectiveness of less than 50 per cent. In late 1940 *Rodney's* sister ship *Nelson* was fitted with a Type 281 air warning radar, which was markedly superior. Not only could it detect aircraft over 100 miles away, it also provided range, bearing and altitude information, and could also detect low-flying aircraft. That winter similar sets were installed in most of the fleet's larger warships, although some, including *Rodney*, made do with a Type 279 set. It was radar that allowed the heavy cruisers *Norfolk* and *Suffolk* to shadow *Bismarck* in May 1941, after the Battle of the Denmark Strait. Without it, this would have been impossible, as the cruisers

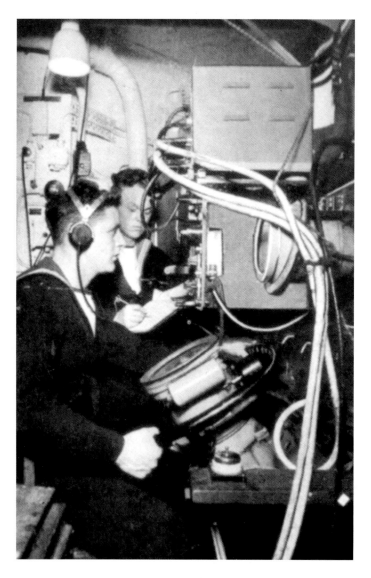

One of the big advantages the Royal Navy enjoyed over the Kriegsmarine was radar. German sets were much less advanced and were more prone to failure. Thanks to sets like this, Rear Admiral Wake-Walker's cruisers were able to shadow *Bismarck* during the battleship's breakout into the Atlantic on 24 May 1941.

would have had to come within range of the battleship's guns.

Developments in surface search radar continued throughout 1940–41, and these Type 272 surface search sets began to enter service in early 1941. These provided a greater range of detection than their predecessors – sometimes up to 20 miles. This proved invaluable at night or in thick weather, and could pick up a target as small as a U-boat. While this capability proved a great boon in the Battle of the Atlantic, it also greatly enhanced the search capabilities of the Home Fleet's vessels. So too did the development of air-to-surface radar systems. By 1941, these had begun to enter service with the Fleet Air Arm, and could be used both to search for enemy ships and to guide air strikes against their target. This could also be achieved through direction provided by surface ships, and by mid-1941 the first fighter direction systems were appearing in the Royal Navy's fleet carriers.

From the perspective of the Commander-in-Chief of the Home Fleet, this provided him with a greatly enhanced search capability, and advance warning of the development of enemy air or surface threats. The development of the third type of radar – fire control – first began in earnest during 1940, beginning with the introduction of two types of centimetric radar – Type 282 controlling short-range anti-aircraft guns, and Type 285 guiding longer-range anti-aircraft batteries. The shortcomings of the anti-aircraft defence of British warships were highlighted during the Norway campaign and the Dunkirk evacuation. The Admiralty's response was to accelerate the development of these new systems. Towards the end of 1940 the Type 284 fire control system for large-calibre guns was tried out in *King George V*, but it proved problematic, largely because surface targets could be targeted only at a range of 10 miles. This was improved during 1941, and a variant had the ability to detect targets at double that range. During the final battle with the *Bismarck* on

27 May 1941, *King George V* was able to detect the German battleship at a range of around 18 miles.

Underwater detection systems also developed considerably as the war progressed. By 1939 Asdic, the Royal Navy's underwater detection system – the equivalent of American 'sonar' – was in general use in the warships of the Home Fleet. Destroyers mounted the Type 128 set in a dome underneath the vessel. Cruisers and some battleships also carried Asdic, usually a Type 132 set, but unlike destroyers who used theirs to hunt down U-boats, in larger ships these were used defensively, to detect a potential U-boat and then alter course to avoid it. Asdic sets emitted a sound wave which had a range of around a mile. If a contact was detected it would bounce back, giving a reading which not only suggested the presence of a U-boat, but also gave some indication of its range and bearing, based on the time the sound wave took to bounce back to the ship.

As the war progressed Asdic sets became more sophisticated, mainly in the way underwater contacts were tracked as they moved. By the summer of 1941, however, these were still in development, as was a form of RDF equipment used to detect enemy radio transmissions. Known in the fleet as High Frequency Direction Finding (HF/DF), but nicknamed 'Huff-Duff', this used a ship- or shore-mounted aerial to detect these transmissions and determine the bearing of the radio signal. If more than one ship detected the signal, these bearings could be triangulated to give the enemy's position. Like RDF, it was Watson-Watt who first developed the system, and the first prototype sets for seagoing use were first installed in March 1941, although these were for experimental purposes. It was the summer of 1941 before the first fully operational HF/DF sets were fitted to warships of the Home Fleet. Until then, this was a form of naval intelligence gathering, which was controlled by the Admiralty and then sent to the Home Fleet's Commander-in-Chief if the information was relevant.

All this technological development made naval operations much more sophisticated than they had been during World War I. However, the fleet commander and his staff were still at the centre of this technological net, where information was gathered, and then orders were issued to other units of the fleet. All of these sources of information, from reconnaissance aircraft, radar, radio intercepts or even visual reports, helped the fleet commander build up a picture of enemy movements, and allowed him to react accordingly. During the *Bismarck* sortie of May 1941 all of these elements were in play, as Admiral Tovey used radar to good effect in shadowing the German battleship, air reconnaissance to relocate the ship when evasion had succeeded, and a naval airstrike to finally cripple the battleship. In the end, the destruction of the *Bismarck* was a job for the Home Fleet's big guns and torpedoes, using methods which had changed little since the Battle of Jutland, fought a quarter of a century before.

HOW THE FLEET OPERATED

ORGANIZATION, DOCTRINE AND COMMAND

The Home Fleet was the main striking force of the Navy, and would remain so until the last year of the war. For much of this period the Mediterranean Fleet was slightly smaller, as the Home Fleet had the greater task of opposing the German Kriegsmarine, while also supporting other operations in the Atlantic, including the safe passage of transatlantic convoys, and the prevention of any amphibious invasion of Britain. Its organization, doctrine and command all reflected these three roles.

Organization

When the war began, the Home Fleet was an extremely powerful force, made up of eight capital ships, six cruisers and 16 destroyers, as well as the smaller vessels listed above. The whole force was commanded by the Commander-in-Chief, Home Fleet, a full Admiral, whose flagship was one of the fleet's most modern battleships. For administrative purposes the flagship formed part of the fleet's main battle squadron, which was commanded by a Rear Admiral, from his own flagship. In practice, the fleet flagship operated independently of his command and never sailed under the command of the battle squadron commander. In this respect the fleet flagship acted in a similar manner to Admiral Jellicoe's flagship, the dreadnought *Iron Duke*, during World War I. At Jutland, *Iron Duke* was placed among the battlefleet as part of a battle squadron, whereas in 1939 the days of massed dreadnoughts had passed and therefore there was no need for *Iron Duke* to fight as part of a squadron.

The Second-in-Command of the Home Fleet was a Vice Admiral, who served as the commander of the fleet's battlecruiser squadron. In addition to being the fleet commander's deputy, he could operate independently, much as his

predecessor Vice Admiral Beatty had done with his Battlecruiser Fleet during World War I. In this role, he could take command of other squadrons and flotillas in the fleet, on an ad hoc basis. These consisted of one or more cruiser squadrons, an aircraft carrier strike force, and destroyer flotillas. During World War II the Home Fleet was regularly formed into temporary groups of this kind, to best suit the operational situation.

FLEET COMPOSITION AT OUTBREAK OF WAR	
2nd Battle Squadron (Rear Admiral Blagrove)	*Royal Oak* (flagship), *Royal Sovereign, Ramillies, Nelson* (fleet flagship), *Rodney*
Battlecruiser Squadron (Vice Admiral Whitworth in *Hood*)	*Hood* (flagship), *Renown, Repulse*
18th Cruiser Squadron (Rear Admiral Hallifax)	*Aurora* (flagship), *Sheffield, Belfast, Edinburgh, Newcastle, Norfolk*
6th Destroyer Flotilla (Captain Nicholson in *Somali*)	8 Tribal-class destroyers 11th Division (4): *Somali* (leader), *Ashanti, Mashona, Matabele*
	12th Division (4): *Punjabi, Tartar, Bedouin, Eskimo*
8th Destroyer Flotilla (Captain Daniel in *Faulknor*)	9 F-class destroyers 15th Division: *Foxhound, Fury, Fearless, Forester*
	16th Division: *Fortune, Fame, Foresight, Firedrake*

The composition of the fleet varied considerably during the years that followed. Although capital ships tended to remain with the Home Fleet for some time, cruisers and destroyers were regularly detached from it for service in other theatres, usually the Mediterranean, or to provide escorts for convoys. From an organizational standpoint this meant that it was almost impossible to maintain this formal pre-war organizational structure. The biggest change came on 14 October 1939. When the battleship *Royal Oak* was torpedoed and sunk in Scapa Flow, Rear Admiral Blagrove, who commanded the Home Fleet's Battle Squadron, went down with his ship. Afterwards, Admiral Forbes made the decision not to replace him, as he saw such formal arrangements as a reflection of the past rather than the future. From that point on, Forbes took direct command of the battleships under his command.

The 2nd Battle Squadron continued to exist as a purely administrative force. However, from that point on commands within the Home Fleet were

The light cruiser *Aurora*, flagship of Rear Admiral Hallifax, at the start of the war. He normally commanded the Home Fleet's destroyers, but when the war began he was temporarily given command of the newly formed 18th CS. In October he ceded the cruiser squadron to Vice Admiral Layton. *Aurora*, an Arethusa-class light cruiser, carried six 6in guns.

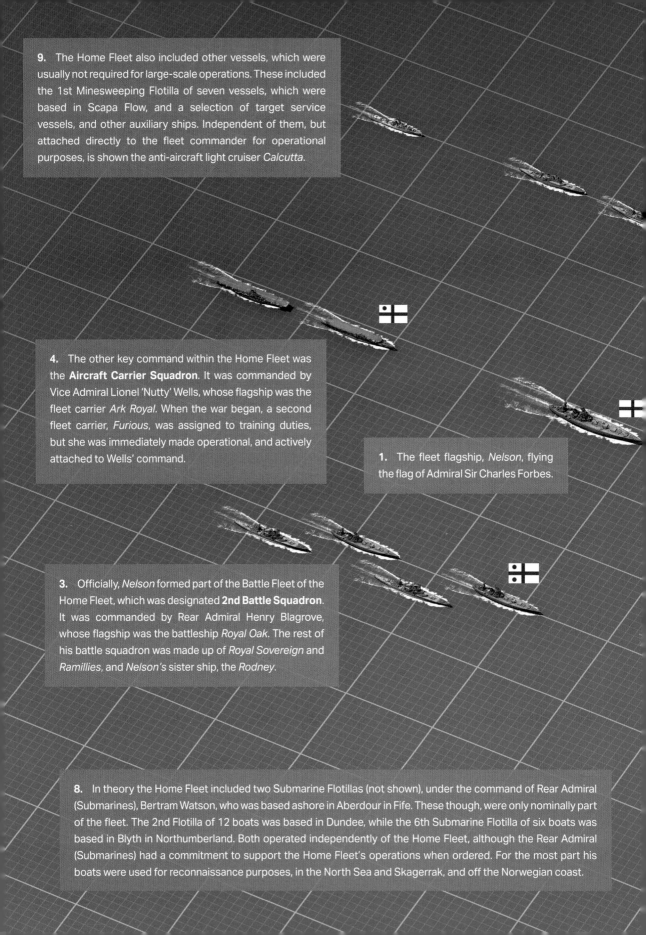

9. The Home Fleet also included other vessels, which were usually not required for large-scale operations. These included the 1st Minesweeping Flotilla of seven vessels, which were based in Scapa Flow, and a selection of target service vessels, and other auxiliary ships. Independent of them, but attached directly to the fleet commander for operational purposes, is shown the anti-aircraft light cruiser *Calcutta*.

4. The other key command within the Home Fleet was the **Aircraft Carrier Squadron**. It was commanded by Vice Admiral Lionel 'Nutty' Wells, whose flagship was the fleet carrier *Ark Royal*. When the war began, a second fleet carrier, *Furious*, was assigned to training duties, but she was immediately made operational, and actively attached to Wells' command.

1. The fleet flagship, *Nelson*, flying the flag of Admiral Sir Charles Forbes.

3. Officially, *Nelson* formed part of the Battle Fleet of the Home Fleet, which was designated **2nd Battle Squadron**. It was commanded by Rear Admiral Henry Blagrove, whose flagship was the battleship *Royal Oak*. The rest of his battle squadron was made up of *Royal Sovereign* and *Ramillies*, and *Nelson's* sister ship, the *Rodney*.

8. In theory the Home Fleet included two Submarine Flotillas (not shown), under the command of Rear Admiral (Submarines), Bertram Watson, who was based ashore in Aberdour in Fife. These though, were only nominally part of the fleet. The 2nd Flotilla of 12 boats was based in Dundee, while the 6th Submarine Flotilla of six boats was based in Blyth in Northumberland. Both operated independently of the Home Fleet, although the Rear Admiral (Submarines) had a commitment to support the Home Fleet's operations when ordered. For the most part his boats were used for reconnaissance purposes, in the North Sea and Skagerrak, and off the Norwegian coast.

THE HOME FLEET 1939

2. Forbes' immediate deputy, Second-in-Command, Home Fleet was Vice Admiral Sir William 'Jock' Whitworth, commander of the fleet's **Battlecruiser Squadron**. He flew his flag in *Hood,* and also commanded *Repulse and Renown*.

6. Two destroyer flotillas were attached, under Rear Admiral (Destroyers), who was based ashore in Lyness. When the war began, this post was vacant, so Hallifax also acted as temporary commander of the destroyers: 16 in all, divided into the 6th and 8th Destroyer Flotillas (DFs). The **6th DF** was led by Captain Randolph Nicholson whose flotilla leader was the Tribal class *Somali*. His flotilla was made up entirely of this class; *Ashanti, Bedouin, Eskimo, Mashona, Matabele, Punjabi* and *Tartar*.

5. The Home Fleet's cruisers were concentrated in the **18th Cruiser Squadron**, under Rear Admiral Ronald Hallifax, who flew his flag in the Arethusa-class light cruiser *Aurora*. Also under his command were four other light cruisers; *Sheffield* and *Newcastle*, both of the Southampton class, and the two Edinburgh-class cruisers *Belfast* and *Edinburgh*. Also in the squadron was the heavy cruiser *Norfolk*, namesake of her class.

7. The **8th DF**, under Captain Charles Daniel in the 'E &F class' flotilla leader *Faulknor*, was made up entirely of 'F class' destroyers; *Fame, Fearless, Firedrake, Foresight, Forester, Fortune, Foxhound* and *Fury*. Each of these two flotillas was sub-divided into two divisions, each of four or five ships.

The Royal Sovereign-class battleship *Royal Oak*, flagship of the Home Fleet's 2nd Battle Squadron. *Royal Oak* flew the flag of Rear Admiral Blagrove. Early on 14 October 1939 the battleship was sunk in Scapa Flow by torpedoes fired from the German U-boat U-47. A total of 834 of the crew were lost.

created on an operational basis. This meant, for instance, that task groups were created to suit the fleet's needs, rather than forming part of a more rigid structure, of the kind used by the Grand Fleet. As for the capital ships, Forbes quickly realized that his two remaining Royal Sovereign-class battleships were too slow to be of much use when it came to intercepting German surface raiders. Accordingly, from that point on they were effectively relegated to second-line duties, usually with the 3rd Battle Squadron, a formation based in Halifax, Nova Scotia. Its primary duty was to provide capital ship escorts for key transatlantic or troopship convoys. The exception was *Resolution*, which was attached to the Home Fleet during the Norway campaign.

The aim was to replace the Royal Sovereign class in the Home Fleet with the modernized battleships of the Queen Elizabeth class. After the sinking of *Royal Oak*, *Warspite* and *Barham* were sent to join the Home Fleet, but the latter was torpedoed, and had to limp into Liverpool for extensive repairs. *Warspite* remained with the Home Fleet until May 1940, and from 6 December 1939, following the damage of *Nelson* and the need for vital repairs for *Rodney*, *Warspite* became the fleet flagship. *Rodney* would succeed to this position the following January, while *Nelson* would assume the role again in August 1940, when her repairs in Portsmouth were completed.

After joining the Home Fleet, *Warspite* was subsequently joined by sister ships *Queen Elizabeth* and *Valiant*. The three Queen Elizabeths formed the core of the fleet under Forbes' direct command until the end of the Norway campaign. It would be the end of the year before the brand-new *King George V* joined the fleet, followed by *Prince of Wales* the following April. By then *King George V* had succeeded *Nelson* as the fleet flagship.

The loss of *Hood* on 24 May 1941 also marked the end of an independent battlecruiser squadron. Any battlecruisers within the Home Fleet would then be controlled directly by the fleet commander. However, the post of Second-in-Command of the Home Fleet would remain, and on 6 June 1941, Vice Admiral Alban Curteis assumed the role, as well as becoming the commander of the 2nd Battle Squadron. For other commands, Rear Admirals in command of cruiser squadrons or even the senior cruiser captain present within a force would often be used to command forces on patrol.

In May 1941, Rear Admiral Wake-Walker, commanding the 1st Cruiser Squadron, would command the heavy cruisers *Norfolk* and *Suffolk* as they patrolled the Denmark Strait. At the same time Captain Madden, as the most senior captain, would command his own cruiser *Birmingham*, as well as *Manchester* and *Arethusa*, as the three light cruisers patrolled the Iceland-Faeroes gap. Meanwhile, Admiral Tovey would take direct command of every other major warship in the Home Fleet, as well as those diverted to join him during the pursuit and sinking of the *Bismarck*.

Doctrine

When the war began there was no clear doctrine in place to govern the actions of the Home Fleet. It was clear that while it had originally been created during the 1930s to perform the same role as the Grand Fleet, another fleet battle was not going to happen. Instead the fleet's primary role was to impose a distant blockade of the Northern Fleet. Between September 1939 and May 1940 the Northern Patrol between Orkney, Shetland and Southern Norway was in place to prevent German merchant ships from passing between the North Sea and the Atlantic Ocean. The Home Fleet's job was to prevent the surface warships of the Kriegsmarine from doing the same. This used the Northern Patrol as a tripwire, to warn of any naval breakout attempt. Light cruisers would be on hand to reinforce the patrol if it was attacked, while the main body of the Home Fleet would remain in Scapa Flow. Its task was to sail out to do battle if the Kriegsmarine attempted a large-scale sortie.

There was no naval doctrine to follow. Instead all operations were designed to support the blockade, and the patrol. The first tripwire was made up of lighter forces from the cruiser divisions and destroyer flotillas. This meant that the cruiser squadron commanders would be the men on the spot. Their job would be to quickly evaluate the strength of the sortie, and then, if required, request the support of the battle fleet. The Northern Patrol actually involved two thin patrol lines, with its ships spaced 8–10 miles apart. The first would usually rely on armed merchant ships or other smaller craft, while the second line tended to be made up of the Home Fleet's cruisers and destroyers.

Forbes' dispositions relied on timely intelligence, allowing him to lead the Home Fleet to sea. It would then sweep to the north of the patrol line, intervening if necessary. If the Germans had brushed past the patrol line, then the Home Fleet would head north, to cover the Faeroes gap. In some cases older,

Rear Admiral Frederick Wake-Walker (1888–1945) assumed command of the Home Fleet's 1st Cruiser Squadron in January 1941. The 1st CS joined the Home Fleet in October 1939. During the *Bismarck* sortie in May 1941, Wake-Walker's cruisers shadowed the enemy battleship after the sinking of the *Hood* in the Denmark Strait.

slower battleships might be stationed to patrol other channels, such as the ones between Orkney and Shetland and Shetland and the Faeroes. In the event of a sortie, other semi-detached forces would be ordered to join the Home Fleet from ports such as Rosyth. Submarines would also be used to patrol the waters at the western end of the Skagerrak, and between the southern tip of Norway and Horn's Reef on the western coast of Denmark. This was a modern war, and Forbes intended to make full use of radio or wireless communications to ensure his ships were in the right place to intercept the Germans.

In addition, support from RAF Coastal Command was expected, and, if they came within reach, air strikes could be launched from HMS *Sparrowhawk*, the Fleet Air Arm airfield in Orkney. A second one, HMS *Tern* became operational later in 1941. Similarly, RAF bomber attacks could be mounted from either Orkney or the north of Scotland. If battle were joined, then the lighter forces would be moved out of the way and the Home Fleet's capital ships would begin a surface action. Forbes, and Tovey after him, were well aware that they didn't even have to sink their opponent. By inflicting sufficient damage, they could force their German counterparts to break off the action. After all, the aim was to prevent them from breaking out into the Atlantic. A damaged German battleship or cruiser in the North Atlantic was a liability, and doomed. However, both commanders realized they might well have sufficient firepower to sink their opponent outright.

During the Norwegian campaign of mid-1940 the Home Fleet actually operated as a battle fleet, along the lines envisaged in pre-war naval doctrine.

THE TRIPWIRE DEFENCE: THE NORTHERN PATROL LINE, 1939–40

In September 1939, the British Admiralty instituted the Northern Patrol – the distant blockade of German ports. As in the previous war, this involved maintaining a blockading line far from the German coast, which prevented German merchant ships or warships from breaking out into the Atlantic or returning home to Germany. At first, old C and D-class cruisers were used, but these were increasingly augmented by a fleet of Armed Merchant Cruisers (AMCs). Although independent of the Home Fleet and based in Kirkwall, it operated closely with the Home Fleet, serving as a tripwire in case of a German naval sortie.

There were two sets of patrol lines. One ran from Iceland down to Orkney, with patrols established in the Faeroes gap between Iceland and the Faeroes, between the Faeroes and Shetland, and in the Fair Isle Channel between Shetland and Orkney. The Home Fleet was responsible for maintaining a patrolling force in the Denmark Strait, between Greenland and Iceland. The second patrol line lay off the coast of southern Norway. It actually consisted of two lines of patrolling vessels, the southerly one acting as a tripwire for the second more northern line. If these detected a sortie by German warships, while other patrolling vessels got out of the way, any cruisers would shadow the enemy, guiding the Home Fleet's battle fleet towards it.

In addition, a submarine patrol was maintained across the western end of the Skagerrak, between Norway and Denmark, and also covering the route from the German North Sea coast to Norway. Finally, RAF Coastal Command maintained regular marine reconnaissance patrols over the North Sea, as well as over the approaches to the Atlantic between Iceland and Orkney.

Atlantic Ocean

Faeroes

Faeroes Gap Patrol

Outer Hebrides

Faeroes-Shetland Patrol

SCOTLAND

Scapa Flow
Orkney

Fair Isle Channel Patrol

Kirkwall

Wick

Fair Isle

Shetland

Lerwick

Aberdeen

RAF Coastal Command Patrols

Norwegian Patrol

North Sea

Bergen

Ålesund

NORWAY

Stavanger

Submarine Patrols

Skagerrak

Trondheim

Kristiansand

FLEET COMMANDERS

Commander-in-Chief, Home Fleet

Admiral Sir Charles Forbes (from April 1938 to December 1940, promoted to Admiral of the Fleet in May 1940). Flagship: *Nelson* (April 1938 to December 1939 and July–December 1940), *Warspite* (December 1939 to January 1940, *Rodney* (January–July 1940)

Admiral Forbes (1880–1960) was an experienced commander, and was well respected in the Admiralty. He had first seen action at the Battle of Jutland (1916), and was a gunnery specialist and former Third Sea Lord. A thorough professional, his one fault was probably his caution, which played a part in his handling of the fleet during the Norwegian campaign (1940).

Admiral John Tovey (from December 1940 to May 1942). Flagship: *Nelson* (December 1940 to March 1941), *Queen Elizabeth* (March–April 1941), *King George V* (April 1941 to May 1942)

Admiral 'Jack' Tovey (1885–1971) distinguished himself in command of a destroyer at Jutland (1916), and he primarily regarded himself as a 'destroyer man'. He was deeply religious, and could be acerbic and intolerant, which earned him the disapproval of the Prime Minister. Nevertheless, he was a highly respected, thoughtful commander, and performed well during the hunt for the *Bismarck*. Like his predecessor, he relaxed while in Orkney by golfing and fishing. He was awarded a knighthood (KCB) in January 1941, with the investiture held that August.

Second in Command, Home Fleet

Post unofficially assumed by Commander, Battlecruiser Squadron (BCS). Officially in November 1940. In June 1941, following the disbandment of the BCS, the post was assumed by the Commander, 2nd Battle Squadron.

Vice Admiral William Whitworth (from November 1940 to May 1941)

Vice Admiral Lancelot Holland (May 1940)

Rear Admiral Alban Curteis (June 1941 to June 1942) (promoted to Acting Vice Admiral in June 1941. Promotion ratified in December)

Commander, Battlecruiser Squadron, Home Fleet

Rear Admiral William Whitworth (from June 1939) (promoted to Vice Admiral in January 1940). Flagship: *Hood* (June 1939 to March 1940), *Renown* (March–April 1940), *Warspite* (April 1940), *Renown* (April–August 1940), *Hood* (August 1940 May 1941)

Vice Admiral Lancelot Holland (from May 1941). Flagship: *Hood* (May 1941). Post ceased to exist with loss of *Hood*, May 1941

Commander, 2nd Battle Squadron, Home Fleet

Rear Admiral Henry Blagrove (from September to October 1939). Flagship: *Royal Oak* (September–October 1939)

Rear Admiral Alban Curteis (June 1941 to June 1942). Flagship: *Dunluce Castle* [base ship] (June 1941 to June 1942), but flag transferred to *Renown* (November–December 1941, January 1942)

Note: Post ceased to exist with loss of *Royal Oak*, October 1939, and was re-established only in June 1941 when Curteis was appointed. By then the post was primarily a staff appointment in Scapa Flow, largely due to the lack of suitable capital ships in the Home Fleet.

Commander, Aircraft Carriers, Home Fleet

Vice Admiral Lionel 'Nutty' Wells (from July 1939 to June 1940). Flagship: *Ark Royal* (July 1939 to June 1940)

Note: Command detached for special operations in South Atlantic and Mediterranean, October 1939 to April 1940, and then permanently transferred to Mediterranean, July 1940. When no Vice Admiral, Carriers available, fleet carriers were commanded directly by the Commander-in-Chief, Home Fleet.

Commander, 18th Cruiser Squadron, Home Fleet

Formation created at outbreak of war by dividing the 2nd Cruiser Squadron (CS) into two – the 2nd CS based in Humber and the 18th CS attached to the Home Fleet.

Rear Admiral Ronald Hallifax (from September to November 1939). Flagship: *Aurora*

Vice Admiral Geoffrey Layton (from November 1939 to June 1940). Flagship: *Aurora* (November to December 1939), *Manchester* (December 1939 to June 1940)

Vice Admiral Frederick Edward-Collins (from June to November 1940). Flagship: *Aurora* (June–October 1940), *Edinburgh* (October–November 1940)

Rear Admiral Lancelot Holland (from November 1940 to May 1941) (promoted to Vice Admiral, January 1941). Flagship: *Birmingham*

Vice Admiral Neville Syfrett (May 1941 to January 1942). Flagship: *Edinburgh*

Note: Hallifax was actually Rear Admiral Destroyers (Home Fleet) when the war began. His command of 18 CS was a temporary appointment. He then resumed his earlier duties.

Commander, 1st Cruiser Squadron, Home Fleet

Transferred to Home Fleet, October 1939

Vice Admiral John Cunningham (from October 1939 to January 1941). Flagship: *Devonshire*

Rear Admiral Frederick Wake-Walker (from January 1941 to February 1942). Flagship: *Devonshire* (January–March 1941), *Norfolk* (March 1941 to February 1942)

Commander, 2nd Cruiser Squadron, Home Fleet

Transferred to Home Fleet, January 1940

Vice Admiral Frederick Edward-Collins (from October 1939 to October 1940). Flagship: *Southampton* (October 1939

to June 1940), *Birmingham* (June–August 1940), *Edinburgh* (August–October 1940)

Rear Admiral Alban Curteis (from October 1940 to June 1941). Flagship: *Galatea*

Rear Admiral Philip Vian (from June to October 1941). Flagship: *Nigeria*

Commander, 15th Cruiser Squadron, Home Fleet

Transferred to Home Fleet, May 1940

Rear Admiral Edward King (from May 1940 to April 1941). Flagship: *Naiad*

Transferred to Mediterranean, July 1940

Commander, 10th Cruiser Squadron, Home Fleet

Transferred to Home Fleet, September 1940

Rear Admiral Harold Burrough (from September 1940 to August 1942). Flagship: *Kenya*

Transferred to Gibraltar, January 1941

Forbes sent his battlecruisers ranging ahead in an attempt to locate and pin the enemy, and intended to use his main battle fleet to decide the issue. It was simply unfortunate that in early May 1940 Forbes was unable to get to grips with the enemy before the Germans had completed their landings. The Royal Naval emphasis on the offensive led directly to the two battles of Narvik – one a probe against a surprisingly powerful opponent, and the second a clinical destruction of a German destroyer flotilla. After that the campaign degenerated in doctrinal terms – the fleet's mission evolved from one of engaging the Kriegsmarine to battle to the support of British land forces in Norway. In this phase, the fleet's warships proved themselves unsuited to operating in the face of heavy enemy air cover.

The real challenge for Forbes was the lack of intelligence on enemy moves. This is what led directly to the sinking of the fleet carrier *Glorious*, and the heroic but doomed last-ditch defence by the destroyer escorts. After the evacuation of Norway and the ceding of the country to the Germans, any operations by the Home Fleet were in response to attempted German breakouts into the North Atlantic. Here, Forbes and his deputy Holland were able to form ad hoc commands, and so deploy in support of their patrols in the Denmark Strait and Faeroes gap. Weather occasionally played a major part in the British failure to prevent German incursions. So too did the distances involved, and the lack of intelligence reports of impending German sorties.

It is ironic that during Operation *Rheinübung*, the sortie of *Bismarck* and *Prinz Eugen*, Admiral Tovey's deployment was faultless. The loss of *Hood* and Vice Admiral Holland along with the ship, was as much down to bad luck than anything else. Certainly Holland's tactics could be questioned, and the weakness

Admiral Sir John 'Jack' Tovey (1885–1971) was given command of the Home Fleet in December 1940, and was knighted in the New Year Honours List a few weeks later. A veteran of Jutland (1916), Tovey was one of the most level-headed naval commanders of the war, and one of the most tenacious.

of his flagship's armour could be raised. On paper though, Holland had the edge, and at the least could have expected to force his counterpart Admiral Lütjens to abandon the breakout, after receiving significant damage to *Bismarck*. Luck, however, was not on Holland's side. Still, it later helped Tovey in that lucky hit from one of *Ark Royal*'s torpedo bombers. It was a last roll of the dice, and in this case it was Lütjens whose luck eluded him. All that remained was for Tovey to finish off the crippled German battleship, using main gun broadsides which would not have been out of place at Jutland, almost exactly a quarter of a century before.

Command

The Home Fleet was under the command of its Commander-in-Chief, a full Admiral, who flew his flag in one of the fleet's battleships. He was answerable to the Admiralty in London, where operational decisions were made by the First Sea Lord. When the flagship was in Scapa Flow, a telephone cable secured to the mooring buoy provided a direct link between the commander-in-chief's office on board and the operations room in the Admiralty. At the outbreak of war on 3 September 1939, the fleet was commanded by Admiral Sir Charles Forbes, a position he had held since 23 April the previous year. On 2 December 1940, he was succeeded by Admiral John Tovey, who held the post until 23 May 1943. Between them, these two admirals shaped the Home Fleet during the key early-war period.

For the most part they commanded the fleet from their flagship, either *Nelson*, *Rodney* or in the case of Tovey *King George V*. The Commander-in-Chief of the Home Fleet was expected to lead his fleet into battle, much as Jellicoe had with the Grand Fleet, so his flagship was well equipped as a floating headquarters. A flagship would have well-appointed cabins for the Admiral and his senior staff in the stern of the ship. In rough weather those in the Nelson class could be extremely uncomfortable, and in especially stormy weather they were uninhabitable due to the motion of the ship. However, the Admiral had his own suite of cabins in the forward superstructure – those in the Nelson class being particularly spacious. The flag captain – the commanding officer of the flagship – had his own bridge, where he could get on with the business of commanding his ship without interference from the embarked admiral. Effectively, in all three of these flagships the Admiral had his own bridge and suite of office cabins in the deck below the captain's bridge.

In the case of *King George V*, Tovey's Admiral's bridge was open to the elements, protected only by an awning, while astern of it in the superstructure was a remote control office, which served as an administrative base, a plotting office, a wireless telegraphy (W/T) office and a chart house. This would be the Commander-in-Chief's base while the ship was in action. The Admiral could conduct the battle from his bridge, but by 1941 he was more likely to rely on information supplied by radar and other sources. More routine administration was conducted from offices below decks in the battleships, where the Admiral also had spacious day cabins and a dining room, as well as a suite of additional offices.

Both Admiral Forbes and Admiral Tovey commanded the Home Fleet through a staff of around two dozen officers and a similar number of ratings. Modern warfare was too complex for one admiral to do everything, therefore he would rely on his Chief of Staff to organize the Fleet's staff and to make sure everything ran smoothly. In Scapa Flow, the Home Fleet also had land-based offices in Lyness. Under the Chief of Staff, usually an officer of flag rank himself, was a small staff responsible for various professional areas of expertise. These included a Fleet Navigating Officer (or Master of the Fleet), Fleet Engineering Officer, Fleet Gunnery Officer, Fleet Anti-Submarine Officer, Fleet Torpedo Officer, Fleet Wireless Officer, Fleet Air Officer and finally the Captain of the Fleet, who oversaw fleet maintenance schedules.

An Operations Staff assisted the admiral with operational planning, while a small administrative team, usually led by the Fleet Accountant Officer, oversaw fleet logistics and personnel. The Commander-in-Chief leaned heavily on his Flag Lieutenant, usually a Commander, who organized the admiral's diary and social calendar, oversaw his meetings and appointments, and who acted as his personal secretary when in action. An Admiral's Secretary – usually a Paymaster Captain – supervised the Admiral's administrative responsibilities. As the role of the fleet expanded, additional staff were housed in HMS *Proserpine,* the shore base in Lyness, while some normally seagoing fleet officers were also moved ashore. It was found that their duties could be performed just as effectively from the shore as at sea. In addition to these officers, the Admiral's

The fleet flagship of Admiral Forbes was the battleship *Nelson,* namesake of this two-ship class. Built during the 1920s, *Nelson*'s ungainly appearance was a result of the design restrictions imposed by the Washington Naval Treaty. However, the battleship's nine 16in guns meant *Nelson* was still an extremely powerful warship.

Conditions in the fleet's warships were often cramped, and in their messdecks Royal Naval ratings still slept in hammocks, much as their forebears had done in the age of Nelson. They also ate in their messdecks, as food was cooked centrally then distributed before consumption.

Staff included a small entourage of ratings such as signallers, plotting room staff, naval clerks, cooks and stewards. In charge of them, traditionally, was the Admiral's Coxswain, usually a senior Chief Petty Officer.

Compared to some land-based commands this was a relatively small organization. For instance, by mid-1941 Western Approaches Command in Liverpool maintained a staff of over 500. By the end of the war this would have doubled to around a thousand staff. Two dozen was a small enough group to help control a fleet. However, every officer in the staff was selected for his expertise in his particular field. Their job was to advise the Admiral when asked, or to raise problems which he might not have considered. Final responsibility, though, for all operational decisions lay with the Home Fleet's Commander-in-Chief himself. The pressures on the Admiral were immense, especially when facing a sortie by major units of the Kriegsmarine, as both Forbes and Tovey had to do.

The stress on Forbes during the Norway campaign is reflected in his official correspondence, particularly when he commented on the surprising effectiveness of German air power. Forbes also had to deal with a rival, Lord Cork, whose own remit overlapped that of the Home Fleet's commander. In this respect Forbes seems to have had little support from his superiors in the Admiralty, who merely expected him to get on with it. This also reflects the problems inherent in gearing up the machinery of naval command in time of war, after decades of peace, and a complacent period of 'Phoney War' in its wake. Tovey, for all his often-fractious relations with the Admiralty, had an easier time of it as he was given unchallenged responsibility to wage the *Bismarck* hunt as he saw fit, and the Admiralty saw its role as a supportive one. It also helped, of course, that Tovey, even more so than Fraser, was very cool-headed and imperturbable. It seemed that as the war went on, the Admiralty was able to learn from its previous experiences and let the Home Fleet's Commander-in-Chief do his job.

INTELLIGENCE AND COMMUNICATION
Intelligence Gathering

More than any other striking force in the Navy, the effectiveness of the Home Fleet depended on high-quality intelligence gathering and on good and timely reports of enemy activity. Fortunately, it could draw on the Admiralty's own intelligence department to supply it with much of this. The rest came from a range of other sources, mainly RAF Coastal Command, its own submarine patrols and, before May 1940, from vessels stationed on the Northern Patrol. The Naval Intelligence Division (NID) was set up in 1912, absorbing an earlier Victorian intelligence department which had a similar remit. In its original form its duties were more concerned with staff work than intelligence gathering, such as the creation of war plans and mobilization schedules as well as gathering of information on potentially rival naval powers. During World War I, however, the NID really came into its own.

Under the guidance of Rear Admiral Oliver, the Head of Naval Intelligence, the NID concentrated on the gathering of intelligence concerning the German High Seas Fleet. At the heart of this was cryptanalysis – the gathering of intelligence from encoded signals. Thanks to the efforts of the staff of Room 40 in the Admiralty, the German naval codes were broken, and valuable information was gathered on enemy naval movements, the effectiveness of German warships and potential operations. Room 40's biggest coup was the decoding of the 'Zimmermann Telegram' in early 1917, which proposed a German alliance with Mexico. This played a part in ensuring the United States' entry into the war.

By war's end the NID had grown substantially, and had become an indispensable wing of the Admiralty. As well as cryptanalysis it also oversaw the censorship of letters sent through the naval postal system and the briefing of foreign naval attachés and official interpreters on the Admiralty's intelligence-gathering requirements. Although its size and importance declined during the inter-war years, by 1939 the NID still boasted a staff of 76 – a mixture of naval officers and civilians skilled in these various tasks. They were commanded by Rear Admiral Godfrey, a mild-mannered man of immense intellect and an analytical mind. His previous job, before his promotion, was commander of the battlecruiser *Repulse*. Later, his personal assistant, Commander Ian Fleming RNVR, would base the character of 'M' on him when writing his James Bond novels. In fact espionage played almost no part in the NID's wartime activities.

However, during the course of the war strong links were formed with resistance movements in occupied Europe, particularly those operating as coast watchers, or based near key German-occupied ports such as Brest, La Rochelle, Copenhagen, Bergen, Trondheim or Narvik. Using hidden radio sets supplied by the British, these resistance fighters could supply the Admiralty with crucial intelligence. For instance, it was Norwegian coast watchers near Kristiansand who spotted the *Bismarck* was at sea, and others at Brest who reported the arrival there of *Scharnhorst* and *Gneisenau*. Although spies and secret agents existed, these were run by other branches of the British military. They would pass

Vice Admiral Lancelot Holland (1887–1941) was appointed to command the Home Fleet's Battlecruiser Squadron in May 1941, taking over from Vice Admiral Whitworth. Just 12 days later he was killed aboard his flagship, the battlecruiser *Hood*, during the Battle of the Denmark Strait.

The fleet carrier *Glorious* joined the Home Fleet in April 1940, after the German invasion of Norway, providing air cover to Allied troops there, and covering the subsequent evacuation from Norway. On 8 June, while returning to Scapa Flow, *Glorious* encountered the German battleships *Gneisenau* and *Scharnhorst*, and was sunk by them, with the loss of most of her crew.

on information to the Admiralty if it reached them. It was a Polish spy in Gotenhafen who reported that *Bismarck* and *Prinz Eugen* had sailed from there in late May 1941.

One problem was that the NID wasn't alone in intelligence gathering. It was, in fact, only one of several British organizations which did much the same kind of work. MI5 was responsible for counterespionage, the hunting of spies and protection of classified information – internal security if you will. MI6, a branch of the Foreign Office, was also known as the Special Intelligence Service. This was the department which conducted espionage and deployed spies. However, it was of a limited size and lacked the budget to really develop its network during the war. In many instances, good intelligence was gathered from the reading of foreign newspapers, listening to enemy radio bulletins or gathering intelligence through diplomatic or business contacts. Another organization, created in mid-1940, was the Special Operations Executive (SOE), which dealt with agents in occupied Europe, including resistance fighters. While there was some friction between it and the NID, it administered the contacts the Admiralty used to glean information on enemy naval activity. In these instances, the SOE ensured these reports were passed directly to the NID.

As in the previous war the main effort of the NID was cryptanalysis. After all, radio intelligence was the most plentiful source of naval intelligence, as well as the most fruitful. In this it shared its efforts with another organization, the Government Code and Cypher Centre. In addition, the other services – the army and the air force – also maintained their own intelligence divisions, which often proved erratic in passing on key information to the NID. The main reason for that was not inter-service friction, but the simple fact that they rarely understood exactly what information was of primary importance to the Admiralty. To coordinate all this, the Joint Intelligence Committee (JIC) was set up in 1939 to coordinate all these organizations and their sources. Its main aim was to prevent any key intelligence from falling through the cracks.

However, they failed to achieve this during the first year of the war. For example, diplomatic warnings from Sweden and Denmark of the planned German invasion of Norway were ignored, as was espionage intelligence from Germany describing plans for this invasion, codenamed Operation *Weserübung*. Even the Admiralty itself was taken by surprise by the invasion. Reports of German naval preparations had reached the NID, but despite warnings by Rear Admiral Godfrey the Admiralty refused to act. The reason was that it felt the Kriegsmarine was unable to carry out such a large and well-coordinated operation, without first gaining control of the sea off Norway. Such a scheme flew in the face of long-established doctrines of sea power. It failed to realize that with air superiority, almost anything was possible. The JIC improved its game after the fall of France. By the autumn of 1940 useful intelligence information was regularly being passed to the Admiralty, by way of the NID. For instance, the Admiralty was able to be kept appraised of construction work and repair work in German shipyards, and therefore able to follow progress on the building of the battleships *Bismarck* and *Tirpitz*, and the repair of *Scharnhorst* and *Gneisenau* after the damage they suffered during the Norway campaign.

Fortunately for the Admiralty, the sharing of information between intelligence services would underpin British cryptanalysis efforts when deciphering German radio intelligence. This method of intelligence information came in a variety of forms. At its most basic was Traffic Analysis. This merely noted the origins of signals, and looked at changes in their volume. A marked increase in Kriegsmarine signals might suggest a major operation was being planned. This might even extend to an understanding of elements within this traffic. For instance, the NID quickly recognized the Morse code prefix used by U-boats to report the sighting of an Allied convoy. A skilled analyst could also detect the hand of a particular German Morse operator, which might, in turn, yield the name of the vessel sending the signal.

A second form of Traffic Analysis was Radio Direction Finding (DF). This involved noting the bearing a signal came from, and hence the direction of the signaller from the DF Station listening in. In 1939, the British had four of these stations around the British Isles, and the number grew steadily as the war progressed. By cross-referencing the bearings, an approximate position could be obtained for the German vessel sending the signal. This was the method by which, on 25 May 1941, Admiral Tovey commanding the Home Fleet was able to discover roughly where the *Bismarck* was, after the battleship had shaken off the British pursuit in mid-Atlantic. So the system worked, if at least two DF stations picked up the transmission. By early 1941, High Frequency Direction Finding (HF/DF, or 'Huff-Duff') systems were starting to be installed in British warships. These achieved the same results, albeit at shorter range, which would greatly boost the Allied ability to detect enemy vessels at sea.

The most fruitful form of radio intelligence was the full cryptanalysis of German signals.

The battleship *King George V*, namesake of that class, was the first modern battleship to join the Home Fleet in December 1940, and duly became the fleet flagship. During the *Bismarck* sortie Admiral Tovey coordinated the pursuit of the German battleship, and on 27 May *King George V* engaged *Bismarck* in a climactic final battle.

In the 1920s the Germans adopted an 'Enigma' electro-mechanical rotor cypher machine which was dubbed unbreakable. In fact the system was first broken by the Poles in 1939, who passed the information on to the British. A code-breaking and cryptanalysis centre was established at Bletchley Park in Buckinghamshire, and work began on breaking the German codes. Each German service had its own system, but the naval Dolphin Code was partially broken by 1940. As a result, from that point the staff at Bletchley garnered a growing quantity of deciphered German naval signals. Just as importantly, as many of the signals were trivial, such as requests for spares, replacement crew or for repair facilities, these were then collated and indexed. Accordingly, when relevant fresh signals were obtained these could be cross-referenced to build up a better picture of the subject vessel, base or naval operation.

This cryptanalysis, codenamed 'Ultra' by the Allies, retained a Top Secret classification throughout the war. Consequently, its circulation within the Admiralty and the NID was limited to prevent the Germans from discovering their codes had been broken. This gave the Admiralty a problem. At all costs it had to avoid revealing its intelligence source, and so counter-measures such as deployments of the Home Fleet or the re-routing of convoys had to be justified by other intelligence sources, or be passed off as random deployment decisions in order to maintain the deception. This, on occasion, inevitably led to placing Allied lives in danger, but that was the high human cost of maintaining such a superb source of intelligence. As a result, it was 1943 before the Kriegsmarine fully realized its Enigma system had been compromised.

Naval Communications

The Home Fleet relied on a range of communication methods, from the most modern to those like flag signals which had been in use in Nelson's Navy. Secure communications were vital in naval warfare, both on the tactical level, between ships in a group, on an operational plane, between the fleet commander and his subordinates, and also strategically, linking him with his superiors in the Admiralty. Inevitably, in World War II this, in the main, involved various forms of electronic communications, although visual signals still had a part to play in tactical communications. This was because these couldn't be intercepted. The Royal Navy used a set of 26 letter flags, ten numeral ones, plus 26 specialist flags, which had specific meanings when hoisted. Visual signals could also be sent by lamp using Morse code. This was more flexible than flags, as it allowed the sending of longer signals, and those which weren't covered in the naval signals book. Similarly, semaphore flags could be used for the same purpose, either using a signaller or in capital ships a semaphore machine.

On a strategic level, the Royal Navy could transmit orders to naval bases and warships by means of radio messages, or in the case of shore bases like Lyness, by landlines or teleprinters. The Admiralty maintained a global system for this, divided into areas, each linked to a specific transmitting station, such as

Bermuda, the Falkland Islands, Simonstown in South Africa or Louisburg in Canada. In the Home Fleet's area, signals were transmitted from a station in Whitehall. In this case the area was sub-divided into three areas: area A covering the North Sea, the Norwegian and Arctic Sea and the English Channel; B the North Atlantic as far west as the Denmark Strait; and C covering the mid-Atlantic. An Admiralty Area Broadcast could be sent to each of these areas, to cover general warnings or the strategic situation, or it could be sent to individual ships or commands. Thousands of messages were sent this way each week, although the most secure were sent by other means.

When the war began, the Royal Navy still made extensive use of wireless telegraphy (W/T). For all sensitive material these wireless signals were encoded. This involved sending messages in Morse code, using a range of frequencies, depending on the distance required. For instance, High Frequency (HF) was used for long-distance messages, while Medium Frequency (MF) could be used when fleets were closer, and ships were reasonably concentrated. For example, during the Norwegian campaign, Admiral Forbes' flagship kept in touch with his fleet and with Scapa Flow using encoded MF signals. The advantage of W/T messages was that they were hard to intercept by enemy direction finders.

Increasingly, Radio Telephone (R/T) was used for fleet communications. Unlike W/T, it didn't require the same skill level for operators and was faster to use, but it was also more prone to misunderstandings arising from messages due to lack of clarity or where a radio operator could not be easily understood. It was also more susceptible to interference by atmospheric conditions. The facilities for R/T increased steadily throughout the war. For example, in 1939 most destroyers had only low- and medium-frequency radio transmission sets, which had a limited range, as described above. Most larger warships had a wider range of receivers though, allowing HF signals to be received. The provision of R/T sets increased as the war progressed, with larger quantities of HF sets

Suffolk was a Kent-class heavy cruiser, mounting eight 8in guns, and joined the Home Fleet in October 1939, but was often seconded on other duties. However, in May 1941 *Suffolk* played a key part in the shadowing of *Bismarck*, using her Type 279 radar.

becoming available. This, for instance, allowed a ship to send sighting reports for much greater distances. During the *Bismarck*'s sortie in May 1941, the cruisers *Norfolk* and *Suffolk* used HF R/T to send sighting reports to Admiral Tovey's flagship *King George V*. These were then passed on by the flagship to the Admiralty.

The way this worked within the Home Fleet was that all ships listened to Admiralty Area Broadcasts, to keep the crew appraised of the general situation. The fleet flagship also monitored Area Broadcasts in the neighbouring areas, such as Area D (the Atlantic seaboard of North America) and Areas X, Y and Z (the Gibraltar Command), so the fleet commander could gain a clearer picture of the overall situation. It was this, for instance, which allowed Tovey to learn that Vice Admiral Somerville's Force H was being sent to support him during the pursuit of the *Bismarck*. Within the ships of the Home Fleet, low and medium W/T or R/T signals were used on preset channels, to reduce the risk of the signals being intercepted.

For signals originating from the fleet flagship, or between it and Whitehall, HF signals were preferred. In addition an MF auxiliary-wave frequency was used for short-range manoeuvring signals between ships in a formation. If a fleet carrier was at sea, it also used a similar MF striking force wave to keep in contact with its aircraft. In the case of convoys, an MF convoy R/T wave was used, usually by the escort commander or convoy commodore, to transmit information within the convoy itself. Finally, an MF naval air wave was used within a naval group if friendly aircraft were operating with it, such as carrier-based fighter protection or strike forces. The fleet flagship or squadron flagship also monitored RAF frequencies, if land-based air support was available.

In practice, what this all meant was that, when at sea, the Home Fleet's warships all received regular Area Broadcasts, so every crew knew the general situation they faced. Within the fleet, the flagship could keep in touch with the Admiralty in London, and the Fleet commander could maintain contact with his squadron commanders, or even individual ships' captains. Nevertheless, signals tended to be sent by W/T at the start of the war, but by the start of 1941 the simple practicalities of R/T made this system more widely used. However, W/T was retained for encoded messages, rather than regular operational or tactical signals.

It meant that the Commander-in-Chief of the Home Fleet was well supported by a communications system when he was at sea, although due to the risk of signals being intercepted, both Admiral Forbes and his successor Admiral Tovey were great believers in the maintenance of radio silence during large-scale naval operations. Nevertheless, when the flagship was moored to 'A' buoy in Scapa Flow, the fleet commander had a direct secure telephone link with the Admiralty. This was invaluable in allowing discussions between him and his superiors in the Admiralty. Orders too, could be sent quickly and securely by means of teleprinter to either the headquarter facilities in Lyness or directly to a teleprinter on board the flagship. Therefore the Home Fleet was well served in terms of communications, whether in its base or at sea. This proved invaluable when it came to conducting the complex long-range search operations the fleet was called upon to carry out in response to German attempts to sortie into the Atlantic. It could even be argued that without this powerful communications network, the pursuit and sinking of the *Bismarck* could never have happened.

Logistics and Facilities

Britain's Home Fleet was inextricably linked with Scapa Flow – the fleet's wartime anchorage in Orkney. It was here that Admiral Jellicoe's Home Fleet was based during World War I, and steamed off to do battle with the German High Seas Fleet at the Battle of Jutland (1916). During the inter-war years the once formidable defences of Scapa Flow were largely dismantled, although during the 1920s the anchorage was still used as a rendezvous for a summer fleet review. Cattle and sheep now grazed among the coastal batteries covering the entrances to Scapa Flow, and the blockships which once sealed the narrower channels into it rusted away, or shifted in winter gales. It was only in early 1936, as the threat of war reappeared, that the Admiralty remembered the old wartime anchorage.

In 1936–37 work began on the construction of a dozen 15,000-ton fuel oil storage tanks at Lyness, on the Orkney island of Hoy. Twelve of these were built, augmenting the five 12,000-ton tanks built in 1917, which were refurbished. In addition a vast underground tank holding 100,000 tons of fuel oil was built on the low hill of Wee Fea overlooking Lyness, and a World War I-era pumping station was refurbished, to control the flow of fuel oil during the refuelling of the Home Fleet's warships. In October 1937 Scapa Flow was designated a 'Category A Defended Port'. Although this was merely a paper designation.

THE HOME FLEET UNDER AIR ATTACK IN SCAPA FLOW, 10 APRIL 1940 (overleaf)

Thanks to intelligence reports, Admiral Forbes was forewarned of the planned German invasion of Norway, and put to sea on 7 April. Three days later Scapa Flow came under heavy air attack from Luftwaffe bombers operating from captured airfields in Southern Norway. The fleet anchorage had been attacked before, but this was the largest German raid of the war. In all, 60 Junkers Ju-88 and Heinkel He-III took part in the attack on 10 April. The raid though, proved a failure, thanks largely to 'The Scapa Barrage'. The numerous shore-based AA batteries in Orkney, together with the ships of the fleet threw up a curtain of fire on a set bearing.

The aim was to create such a concentrated volume of flak that the bombers would be unable to penetrate it. As a result the bombers were forced to drop their bombs at a hopelessly high height, rendering their attack ineffective. The attackers had also been detected by Chain Link Radar, and fighters were scrambled from RAF Wick in time to attack the Luftwaffe formations as they withdrew. However, almost all of the Home Fleet was at sea off Norway, so the anchorage was virtually empty, save for the heavy cruiser *Suffolk* and the small aircraft carrier *Argus*. Both are seen here, adding their weight to the barrage.

The Tribal-class destroyer *Tartar*, pictured moored in Scapa Flow. Typically, destroyers were berthed away from the main fleet anchorage, between the island of Flotta and the main naval base at Lyness on the island of Hoy. Note the barrage balloon, one of many deployed to protect the fleet from air attack.

Apart from the addition of some anti-submarine nets and booms, the anchorage was completely undefended.

Admiral Forbes had reservations about the suitability of Scapa Flow as a base, but he recognized its immense strategic potential. Therefore, as the war clouds loomed, he encouraged the Admiralty to accelerate the building up of the base's defences. In 1938, following an RAF estimate that the Luftwaffe could drop 450 tons of bombs over the anchorage per day, two fighter squadrons were moved north to Wick on the Scottish mainland, and early the following year heavy AA guns and World War I-vintage coastal defence guns were emplaced in Orkney. During 1939 the defences began taking shape. A Fleet Air Arm airfield, HMS *Sparrowhawk*, was established at Hatston outside Kirkwall, while additional facilities for the fleet were provided, including a direct phone line on 'A' buoy, serving the fleet flagship, which linked it directly to the Admiralty. Additionally, a radar station was established at Netherbutton on Orkney's east mainland, to provide early warning of German air attacks.

On the declaration of war on 3 September 1939, the Admiralty instituted 'Plan Q', its blueprint for the wartime defence of Scapa Flow. The aim was to render the base impenetrable to German U-boats and surface warships, and to make the air defences so formidable that the Luftwaffe would be deterred from attempting air attacks on the anchorage. Additional heavy AA guns were sent to Orkney, and a brigade-sized army garrison was moved there, commanded by Brigadier Kemp, Commanding Officer, Orkney and Shetland Defences (OSDef). For the Navy, the fleet support facilities and the defence of the base itself fell under the control of a new naval command, based on board the obsolete dreadnought *Iron Duke*, which was moored in Scapa Flow near Lyness. It duly became the flagship of Admiral French, Admiral Commanding, Orkney and Shetland (ACOS).

In addition, Vice Admiral Horton, who commanded the Northern Patrol, established his headquarters in Kirkwall, Orkney's largest town. As the first

Luftwaffe reconnaissance flights reached Scapa Flow, Admiral French and Brigadier Kemp worked to improve the still very basic anchorage defences. One of the most immediate problems was the sealing up of Scapa Flow. While the main entrance at Hoxa Sound was reasonably secure, as was the secondary one in Hoy Sound, the situation was less satisfactory on the eastern side of the Flow, where three small channels – Kirk Sound, Weddel Sound and Water Sound – provided a potential entry route for U-boats or German light surface warships. During World War I these sounds had been sealed by blockships – old merchant ships filled with concrete, and scuttled to block the channel.

Many of these had shifted in the intervening years, and so their effectiveness was now questionable. A handful of new merchant ships were sourced by the Admiralty and sent to Orkney to be used as blockships. By mid-October all but the more northerly channel, Kirk Sound, had been rendered impassable. The 4,000-ton steamer SS *Neuchatel* was earmarked to seal this channel, but was still not in place when disaster struck. On the night of 13/14 October, Kapitänleutnant Gunther Prien commanding U-47 slipped through the channel on the surface and successfully entered Scapa Flow. Prien's U-boat had been specially selected for the mission, and the latest Luftwaffe reconnaissance photographs showed that Kirk Sound was still unblocked. A raid was set in motion.

Prien had left Kiel on 8 October and arrived off the eastern side of Orkney five days later. He made the passage through Kirk Sound in the early evening, at high tide, and despite briefly snagging on the mooring cable of a blockship U-47 made it through safely and undetected. He found the main anchorage was empty – Admiral Forbes and the bulk of the Home Fleet were at sea. However, in the northern portion of the Flow, Prien sighted the Royal Sovereign-class battleship *Royal Oak*, anchored a mile off the craggy eastern shore of Scapa Bay. *Royal Oak* had returned to Orkney early on 11 October, having being patrolling to the west of Shetland, acting as a 'backstop' for the Home Fleet during a possible sortie by the German battleship *Gneisenau*. On 13–14 October, *Royal Oak* was providing AA defence for the Netherbutton radar station. Seizing his opportunity, Prien closed in.

One of U-47's first spread of torpedoes hit but caused relatively inconsequential damage. After reloading, at 0112hrs Prien fired his second spread. Two of the three hit amidships with devastating effect. *Royal Oak* listed heavily to starboard, and five minutes later capsized, trapping many of the crew inside the hull. In all, 834 men and boys died on board the battleship.

By then Prien was heading back towards Kirk Sound. He made his way out of Scapa Flow without incident, as behind him destroyers hunted in vain for the U-boat. In Scapa Flow, after all rescue attempts were completed, a Board of Enquiry was convened in Lyness on 18 October, as the Admiralty demanded answers. How could such a disaster happen in what was meant to be a secure anchorage? Captain Benn of *Royal Oak* and Rear Admiral

After returning safely to Wilhelmshaven, Prien and his men received a tumultuous welcome. After being met by Vizeadmiral Dönitz, commanding the Kriegsmarine's U-boats, Prien was taken to Berlin to meet Hitler. For the Germans, the sinking of the *Royal Oak* in Scapa Flow itself was a major propaganda coup.

Blagrove, commanding the Home Fleet's 2nd Battle Squadron, both died when the battleship sank. Other witnesses testified to the sequence of events, and it was proved conclusively that the battleship had been torpedoed by a U-boat.

It was still unclear to the British how Prien had entered Scapa Flow, but Admiral French was fairly certain which entrance had been used. As he put it: 'Kirk Sound was definitely not impregnable, although extremely difficult, due to the strength of the tide.'

By the end of the enquiry the weaknesses of Scapa Flow's defences had been laid bare. Not only were there gaps in the lines of blockships protecting the eastern entrances, but the main boom defences in the two principal entrances were too insubstantial, while a lack of suitable gun batteries or searchlights was also highlighted as a serious concern. As if to underline these shortcomings, at dawn on 17 October four Luftwaffe Ju 88s penetrated the air defences of Scapa Flow, and bombed the old dreadnought *Iron Duke* lying off Lyness. Jellicoe's old flagship from Jutland was now just a depot ship, but held historical significance. *Iron Duke* was damaged below the waterline, and had to be beached to prevent her from sinking. This underlined the point that Scapa Flow was poorly protected, despite the Admiralty's claims.

This came as no surprise to Admiral Forbes. As early as 1 October, he had taken his flagship out of Scapa Flow, accompanied by *Rodney, Hood, Repulse* and *Ark Royal*, and established a temporary base at Loch Ewe, beyond the reach of enemy bombers. Although they would return to Scapa Flow occasionally, he essentially abandoned the base until its defences were markedly improved. So, throughout the winter Admiral French and newly promoted Major General Kemp set about making this happen. By 11 March 1940, Churchill was able to tell the House of Commons that Scapa Flow 'was 80 per cent secure'.

By then the three eastern sounds had been plugged by blockships, and their approaches covered by coastal batteries and searchlights. The defences of the main entrances at Hoxa Sound and Hoy Sound had been greatly strengthened, with large coastal batteries, improved anti-submarine boom defences, searchlight positions, underwater induction loops to detect U-boats, controlled minefields and anti-torpedo nets. Other batteries covered the approaches to Kirkwall, headquarters of the Northern Patrol. As for air defence, there were now 16 heavy AA batteries around Scapa Flow, and two RAF and one Fleet Air Arm airfields were now operational, augmenting the RAF airfield at Wick on the Scottish mainland. A Second Fleet Air Arm airfield would become operational in mid-1941. In addition, the radar station at Netherbutton had been augmented by several more, ensuring excellent forewarning of any German air attack. Scapa Flow was now secure enough for Admiral Forbes to lead the Home Fleet back to its main wartime base.

As *Nelson* was under repair after striking a mine, Forbes flew his flag in *Rodney* when he led the Home Fleet back to Scapa Flow on 9 March 1940. That afternoon a meeting was held with Churchill, Forbes, French and various others, to review the state of the base defences. These were deemed satisfactory, although several deficiencies were noted. At the meeting, the decision was also made to solve the problem with the eastern channels by building a causeway, linking the four islands there to the Orkney mainland. This large civil engineering project would result in the construction of the Churchill Barriers, built by a combination of civil construction companies and Italian prisoners of war. To prevent this from being deemed a warlike project, the decision was made to top the barriers with a road, permanently linking the inhabited islands of Burray and South Ronaldsay to the Orkney mainland. However, it would be 1 May 1945 before the Churchill Barriers were officially opened to civilian traffic. They have remained in use ever since.

As a fleet base Scapa Flow was the perfect location, but for many of the sailors and the other servicemen stationed there, it was a grim place with little in the way of shore entertainment, and had long dark winters where gales could last for a week or more. Nevertheless, Lyness grew into a sizeable shore base, named HMS *Proserpine*, which became the headquarters of ACOS. It developed into a major command and communications centre, serving the Home Fleet and linking it to the Admiralty. Many of its staff were Women's Royal Naval Service (WRNS) personnel. The base harbour facilities first constructed during World War I were greatly expanded, including the building of a 600ft-long quayside, capable of taking the largest ships in the fleet. Lyness also boasted a sizeable repair base, as well as facilities to maintain Scapa Flow's boom defences.

At Lyness, damaged warships could be brought alongside the quay and repaired sufficiently for them to then be transferred to other larger shipyards on the British mainland, or even overseas. Lyness was never anything more than a frontline repair facility, although small tasks, such as repairs to storm-damaged ships or other minor repairs could be completed there. For the ships of the Home Fleet, Lyness was a base for refuelling and repairs. For the crews though, it was something more. There were functional but basic bars and cafeterias there, and both in Lyness and the neighbouring island of Flotta

A Luftwaffe reconnaissance photograph, taken in early 1941, showing the line of blockships used to block two of the eastern entrances into Scapa Flow, on either side of the small island of Lamb Holm. The top channel, Kirk Sound, between Lamb Holm and the Orkney mainland, was used by Kapitänleutnant Gunther Prien in U-47 when he raided the anchorage on 13–14 October 1939, and sank the battleship *Royal Oak*.

there were entertainment facilities, such as a garrison theatre and a cinema. There were also football and rugby pitches and a golf course.

This became the recreational centre for thousands of servicemen. Lyness became the true hub of the anchorage, and the epicentre of Home Fleet activities. If lucky, sailors could acquire a pass to travel to Kirkwall, where other facilities were available, including cinemas, pubs and dance halls. Getting leave represented more of a challenge. A regular ferry transported sailors and other service personnel going on leave to Scrabster in Caithness, on the far side of the Pentland Firth. From nearby Thurso they could then travel south by train; although this 'Jellicoe Express' to Inverness was overcrowded, the journey was a lengthy one and facilities were basic. Still, for most it represented their only physical link with their family.

For the most part, the Commander-in-Chief, Home Fleet and his staff remained aloof, controlling operations from the flagship, moored for much of the time on 'A' Buoy. Above all, Scapa Flow existed as a spacious anchorage for the Home Fleet, where ships and crews were safe from attack. Sure enough, during the Luftwaffe air attacks of March and April 1940, the base was deemed as safe from air attack as it was from enemy surface ships or U-boats. This sense of security it afforded to the men of the Home Fleet was the real benefit of the heavily fortified anchorage that was Scapa Flow.

Throughout the war, Royal Navy sailors over the age of 18 were still entitled to a daily rum ration, drawn at 1100hrs each day under the supervision of officers and senior rates. Most ratings drank their ration of ⅛ of a pint watered down, with one part of rum to three parts of water.

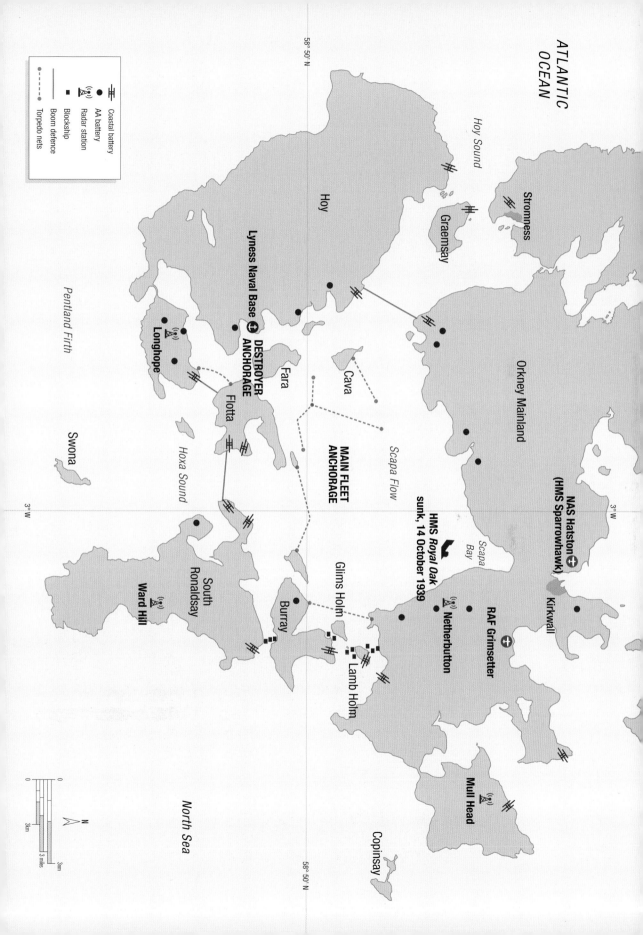

COMBAT AND ANALYSIS

THE FLEET IN COMBAT

While this chapter tells of the fleet's actions, this is not its main emphasis. First, the Home Fleet never performed its operational duties as an integrated whole. Instead, the wartime Home Fleet was often involved in a number of simultaneous operations, and so its fighting strength was often scattered in the Atlantic Ocean, and the Arctic, North and Norwegian seas. While individual actions will be outlined here, the main aim is to capture something of the way the fleet was commanded and deployed during these operations. This will reflect the challenges facing the Commander-in-Chief of the Home Fleet during this period, and show how he made use of the often-scattered resources under his command.

The 'Phoney War'

When the war began on 3 September 1939 the Home Fleet was already at sea, enforcing the blockade of Germany. Submarines were stationed off the entrances to Wilhelmshaven and the Kiel Canal, and cruisers and destroyers were establishing the patrol line between the Scottish and Norwegian coasts. While the light cruisers *Southampton* and *Glasgow* were patrolling off southern Norway at the outbreak of war, Admiral Forbes and the main body of the fleet put to sea in search of the German liner *Bremen*, but the liner evaded Forbes by putting in to Murmansk. After returning to Scapa Flow to refuel, Forbes put to sea again on 7 September, with *Nelson*, *Rodney*, *Repulse*, *Ark Royal*, two light cruisers and ten destroyers. The fleet patrolled off the Norwegian coast, but failed to encounter any Kriegsmarine units. The following day *Hood* and *Renown*, two light cruisers and another four destroyers left to form a second line in the Faeroes gap. Effectively, this was an almost complete deployment of the main units of the Home Fleet.

This was all part of the Royal Navy's strategic goal of establishing maritime control over the approaches to the Atlantic. Control of sea communications beyond this blockading zone was vital to Britain's interests, and in 1939–40, when the blockade of German ports was first established, Forbes nursed a hope that the Germans would come out and contest British maritime control, or at least attempt to break through his blockading forces, to begin commerce-raiding operations in the Atlantic. Therefore, throughout the rest of the year this emphasis on large-scale deployments continued, particularly if there was credible intelligence of a German sortie by capital ships or 'pocket battleships' – the British term for the Kriegsmarine's armoured cruisers. The Home Fleet was also involved in sweeps, such as one into the Skagerrak in late September, or regular patrols off the Norwegian coast.

An example of this was the operation on 8–10 October, in response to a sortie by the German battleship *Gneisenau*. On 8 October *Gneisenau* sailed in company with the light cruiser *Köln* and nine destroyers, and began a sweep off southern Norway. Forbes was warned, and at 1320hrs on 8 October the German force was spotted by a Coastal Command aircraft as it steamed past Kristiansand. That evening Forbes put to sea with the battleships *Nelson* and *Rodney*, the fleet carrier *Furious*, a light cruiser and eight destroyers. His intent was to take up position to the north-east of Shetland. The battleship *Royal Oak* and two destroyers patrolled off Fair Isle, while the battlecruisers *Hood* and *Repulse*, with two light cruisers and four destroyers in company, headed to the waters off Bergen. Finally, the Humber Force of light cruisers and destroyers would patrol the Skagerrak in case the Germans doubled back into the Baltic. Effectively, Forbes and his fleet were laying an ambush.

When the war began, the new fleet carrier *Ark Royal* was the only fully operational carrier in the Home Fleet. A second one, *Furious*, was being used for air crew training, but was swiftly brought into front-line service, giving Forbes two powerful aircraft carriers to support his fleet's operations.

Liberty men from the old battleship *Royal Oak* going ashore to Scapa Pier near Kirkwall on 13 October 1939. That night, most of these men would be killed when the battleship was torpedoed, as *Royal Oak* capsized and sank in a matter of minutes, trapping most of them below decks.

However, that night *Gneisenau* and the group of accompanying ships reversed course, and returned through the Skagerrak to reach Kiel in the early hours of 10 October. Unfortunately for Admiral Forbes, the failure of this speedily planned but well-thought-out ambush was typical of several such operations conducted by the Home Fleet during the first eight months of the war. Afterwards, Forbes took the bulk of his fleet to Loch Ewe – leaving only *Royal Oak* in Scapa Flow, where the ship's anti-aircraft guns were used to protect Orkney's main radio direction finding (radar) station a few miles south of Kirkwall. This meant *Royal Oak* was the only capital ship in the anchorage when U-47 successfully penetrated Scapa Flow's defences and sank the old battleship with heavy loss of life on the night of 13/14 October. Afterwards, Forbes remained in Loch Ewe with the bulk of the fleet until the defences of Scapa Flow were improved.

In late October Forbes was ordered to protect an iron ore convoy sailing between Narvik and the Firth of Forth. This time he used *Nelson*, *Rodney* and *Hood*, plus six destroyers – more than a match for the two German battleships if they sortied again. The convoy arrived unmolested, as did a second one in mid-November. However, on 21 November *Scharnhorst* and *Gneisenau*, under the command of Vizeadmiral Marschall, sailed from Wilhelmshaven, and passed into the Norwegian Sea without being detected by the Northern Patrol. Similarly, British naval intelligence hadn't been forewarned of the German operation. Consequently, Forbes was unprepared, and was in the Clyde, having just returned there after escorting this second convoy. Forbes first learned of the German operation in the afternoon of 23 November, when one of the enemy battleships was sighted to the north of the Faeroes by the auxiliary cruiser HMS *Rawalpindi*. Captain Kennedy of *Rawalpindi* mistakenly identified the battleship as a 'pocket battleship'. In any case, before *Rawalpindi* could escape, the cruiser was sunk by *Scharnhorst's* guns.

In Loch Ewe, Forbes suspected the Germans were attempting a breakout into the North Atlantic, so he deployed his forces accordingly. That evening he left the Clyde with *Nelson* and *Rodney*, accompanied by the heavy cruiser *Dorsetshire* and seven destroyers. Four light cruisers were already in position between Iceland and the Faeroes, while the heavy cruisers *Norfolk* and *Suffolk* blocking the Denmark Strait headed east to reinforce them. While these cruisers were too light to engage the German battleships, they could shadow them, giving Forbes a chance to intercept the German force with his two slow-moving battleships.

Submarines were sent to block the western approaches of the Skagerrak, while three more light cruisers and three destroyers left Rosyth that evening to block the Fair Isle channel. Another five-strong light cruiser force was assembled to block the Faeroes to Shetland gap, while other warships – *Warspite*, *Hood*, *Repulse and Furious*, together with the French battleship *Dunkerque* – were pulled from convoys or other duties and sent to the waters around Iceland and the Faeroes. It was an impressive ad hoc assemblage, but it put to sea too late to stop the Germans reaching the Atlantic. However, Marschall was only probing the Home Fleet's defences. In the evening of 23 November Marschall withdrew into the Arctic Sea, and waited there until he deemed it the right time to make a break for home.

By the afternoon of 25 November, Forbes and his battle squadron were east of the Faeroes and north of Shetland, waiting for news. Elsewhere, all the cruiser

An artist's impression of the wreck of the battleship *Royal Oak*, lying in shallow water in the north-east corner of Scapa Flow, just a mile from the shore. *Royal Oak* capsized on sinking, entombing almost two-thirds of her crew, and their remains still lie there, protected as a war grave.

screens were in place, and also waiting to make contact, but Marschall was still to the north of Forbes, and deemed weather conditions were right to screen his return south only at dawn the following morning. By then Forbes had established a new patrol line off the Norwegian coast, to the north of Bergen. However, Marschall used the poor visibility to slip through the British patrol line, and reached Wilhelmshaven in the afternoon of 27 November. Unaware he had been sidestepped, Forbes remained at sea until late on 29 November, at which point he called off the operation. Even then, on 4 December, *Nelson* hit a magnetic mine on entering Loch Ewe, and was sent back to Portsmouth for repairs. This mine – one of 18 laid across the mouth of Loch Ewe – showed that the Germans were well aware the Home Fleet was using this natural harbour as a base while Scapa Flow was being rendered impregnable.

For the remainder of 1939 and into 1940 the Home Fleet was based in the Clyde, and continued to cover the channels leading into the North Atlantic, despite the ferocious weather. The fleet also provided powerful escorts for transatlantic troop convoys and for Norwegian ore shipments. Forbes and his men had performed well, despite having no victories to show for all their

FLEET RECONNAISSANCE: HUNTING THE KRIEGSMARINE, NORWAY APRIL 1940

In response to reports that the Germans were attempting to invade Norway, the Home Fleet sailed from Scapa Flow at 2015hrs on 7 April 1940. It was led by Admiral Forbes, flying his flag in the battleship *Nelson*. The Battlecruiser Squadron under Vice Admiral Whitworth, flying his flag in the battlecruiser *Renown*, had already sailed, his flagship escorted by four destroyers from the 2nd Flotilla. This was essentially a large-scale sweep of the Norwegian coast, begun at a time when the political and military situation in Norway was still unclear. Contact was first made early on 8 April, when the destroyer *Glowworm*, detached from Whitworth's screen, encountered the German heavy cruiser *Admiral Hipper*, and was sunk after ramming the larger opponent. Early on 9 April, off the Lofoten Islands, *Renown* briefly engaged the German battleships *Gneisenau* and *Scharnhorst*.

After contact was lost due to the atrocious weather, Forbes ordered Whitworth, who had been reinforced by the battlecruiser *Renown*, to patrol off the entrance to the Vestfjord, which led to Narvik. Meanwhile he led the battle fleet northwards, in a sweep up the Norwegian coast.

The aim was to catch the German naval groups between these two British pincers. In both forces the main body was preceded by a screen, some 10–15 miles in front of the flagship. These were expected to detect the enemy and maintain contact until the capital ships could join them. Forbes also sent two cruiser squadrons in a sweep down the coast as far as Stavanger. These reconnaissance tactics were similar to those practised during World War I. To improve their chances both Forbes and Whitworth launched floatplanes to scout ahead of their force. Forbes also had the fleet carrier *Furious*. Early on 11 April the carrier's Swordfish aircraft launched a sweep over Trondheim, where *Hipper* had last been sighted. This failed to find any targets, and elsewhere the seas seemed devoid of the Germans. In fact almost all of the German naval forces had already returned home, save a destroyer flotilla off Narvik, which was attacked by Whitworth's destroyers on 10 April. Forbes had been singularly unlucky. His fleet reconnaissance had failed to find the enemy. All that was left for him was the annihilation of those German destroyers, which was completed on 13 April.

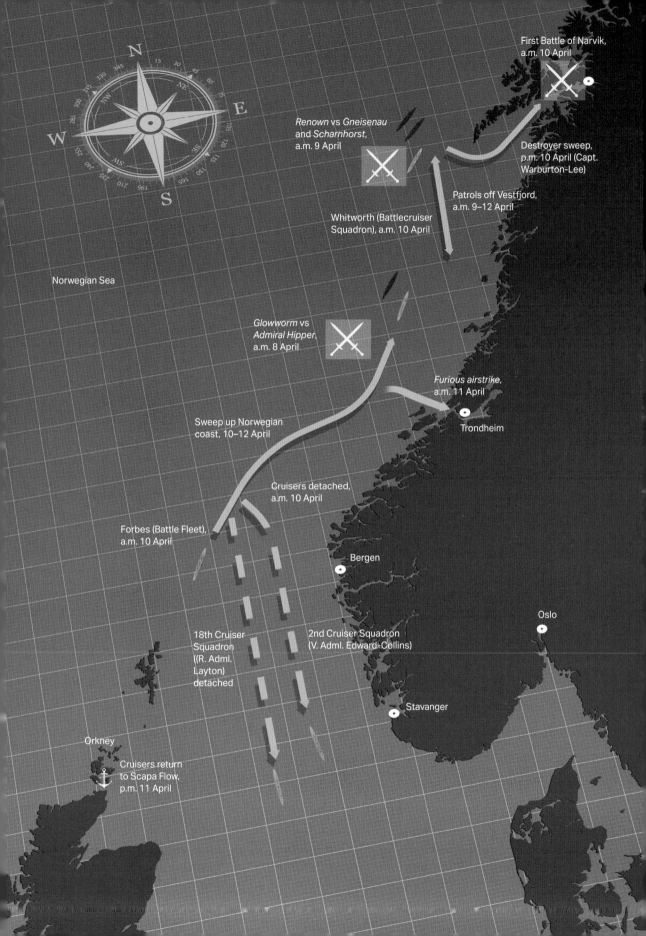

First Battle of Narvik,
a.m. 10 April

Renown vs *Gneisenau*
and *Scharnhorst*,
a.m. 9 April

Destroyer sweep,
p.m. 10 April (Capt.
Warburton-Lee)

Whitworth (Battlecruiser
Squadron), a.m. 10 April

Patrols off Vestfjord,
a.m. 9–12 April

Norwegian Sea

Glowworm vs
Admiral Hipper,
a.m. 8 April

Furious airstrike,
a.m. 11 April

Trondheim

Sweep up Norwegian
coast, 10–12 April

Cruisers detached,
a.m. 10 April

Forbes (Battle Fleet),
a.m. 10 April

Bergen

Oslo

18th Cruiser
Squadron
((R. Adml.
Layton)
detached

2nd Cruiser Squadron
(V. Adml. Edward-Collins)

Stavanger

Orkney

Cruisers return
to Scapa Flow,
p.m. 11 April

efforts. This included nearly continuous sea time, often in stormy conditions, which took its toll on ships and men alike. The Northern Patrol continued, but despite around a hundred merchant ships a month being stopped, only a handful proved to be German. However, the capture of the German supply ship *Altmark* provided a welcome boost to morale. The ship had been supporting the armoured cruiser *Graf Spee*'s commerce-raiding cruise in the South Atlantic, but in late January *Altmark* slipped through the Iceland-Faeroes gap to reach Norwegian waters. On 17 February the supply ship was located and attacked by the destroyer *Cossack*, whose boarding party recovered 299 British prisoners – the crews of *Graf Spee*'s victims. The boarding party's cry of 'The Navy's here!' was repeated with delight by the British press.

Forbes soon faced a far more serious situation. On 18 February, following RAF reports that *Scharnhorst*, *Gneisenau* and the heavy cruiser *Admiral Hipper* had been spotted off Helgoland, Forbes put to sea from the Clyde. However, the sortie never happened as two days later Vizeadmiral Marschall returned to Wilhelmshaven. It was clear that the Germans appeared to be preparing for some kind of large-scale operation – either an Atlantic sortie or another sweep into the Norwegian Sea. In fact, this major operation would not take place until early April. Forbes was merely facing the preparations and training exercise that preceded this fresh German offensive. When it came, it would plunge the Home Fleet into a bitterly fought contest, and would alter the whole strategic situation in northern waters.

The Norwegian Campaign

Both Britain and Germany relied on the import of Swedish iron ore. During 'The Phoney War' the Home Fleet had been involved in the protection of iron ore convoys from the Norwegian port of Narvik to British ports. In summer the Germans transported their ore from Sweden to Germany through the Baltic. In winter, when the Swedish port of Luleå in the Gulf of Bothnia was closed by ice, the Germans were forced to use the Narvik route, their convoys sailing south through Norway's coastal waters to the Skagerrak. In early 1940, the British devised a plan to mine this coastal route, even though Norway was a neutral country. As the *Altmark* incident had proved, the Germans had already breached Norwegian neutrality. This scheme, codenamed Operation *Wilfred*, was due to be implemented in early April 1940. However, it was overtaken by events.

Unknown to the British, a month before, Hitler had approved plans for Operation *Weserübung* ('Weser Exercise'), a German invasion of Denmark and Norway. Seven infantry divisions would be used, together with considerable Luftwaffe assets. In the wave against Norway, near-simultaneous amphibious landings would take place at Narvik, Trondheim, Bergen, Egersund, Kristiansand and Oslo. These six landing groups would be protected by the bulk of the Kriegsmarine. In all, Grossadmiral Raeder committed 14 destroyers, eight torpedo boats and four minesweepers to this task, supported by eight cruisers, including the armoured cruiser *Lützow* and the heavy cruisers *Blücher* and *Admiral Hipper*. Five smaller naval forces would carry out further landings in Denmark, in support of the main invasion across the Danish–German border.

A new fleet commander, Vizeadmiral Lütjens, flying his flag in the battleship *Gneisenau*, would command the covering force in Norwegian waters. It was made up of his flagship with her consort *Scharnhorst*, escorted by a handful of destroyers. These two battleships were there to protect the invasion groups from interference by the Home Fleet, and to be ready to provide additional firepower if they were needed. Finally, 28 U-boats were earmarked to support the operation, operating off the Norwegian and British coasts. The invasion was scheduled to begin on Sunday 7 April 1940.

Fortunately for the British, although their intelligence system failed to forewarn them, at least the Home Fleet was largely ready for action. This had more to do with Operation *Wilfred* than anything else. However, as well as the planned laying of three minefields near Narvik and Trondheim, the British were also holding military forces in readiness. Plan 'R4' called for British landings in Narvik, Trondheim, Bergen and Stavanger, in the event of any German counter-move or breach of Norwegian neutrality. These forces were ostensibly there to support the Norwegians, in the face of a possible German invasion. Landing forces were assembled in the Firth of Forth and the Clyde, ready for deployment if required. Meanwhile, on Friday 5 April an auxiliary minelayer left Scapa Flow, escorted by four destroyers, and the following morning it was followed by a second minelaying group accompanied by four more destroyers. Vice Admiral Whitworth's covering force – the battlecruiser *Renown* and four destroyers – also left Scapa Flow late on 5 April. Neither side was yet aware that the enemy were also heading into the same Norwegian waters.

Whitworth's force reached the Vestfjord – the approach to Narvik – late on 7 April. The minelayers completed their mission that night and returned to Scapa Flow. Whitworth remained at sea off the Lofoten Islands, in response to an Admiralty report that the Germans were mounting some form of major operation. This report also led Admiral Forbes to put to sea with the bulk of the Home Fleet. On Sunday night he left Scapa Flow in his flagship *Rodney*, accompanied by the battleship *Valiant*, the battlecruiser *Repulse*, the cruisers *Sheffield* and *Penelope*, and ten destroyers. In the North Sea they were joined by the French cruiser *Emile Bertin* and two destroyers, and then by Vice Admiral Edward-Collins' 2nd Cruiser Squadron – the light cruisers *Galatea* and *Arethusa* and four more destroyers. Several other light cruisers and destroyers on convoy escort duties were also in the area and could be called upon by Forbes if needed.

Admiralty intelligence, however, was faulty – although Forbes knew there was increased Kriegsmarine activity, he had no idea they were heading towards Norway. First contact with the enemy was made by accident. During the night of 7/8 April, Lieutenant Commander Roope's destroyer HMS *Glowworm*, lost a man overboard and was detached from *Renown*'s screen while an unsuccessful

The final moments of the 'G&H-clasps' destroyer *Glowworm*, laying a smokescreen after trying to torpedo the German heavy cruiser *Admiral Hipper* off Norway on 8 April 1940. Moments later, *Glowworm*'s commander rammed the *Hipper*, causing heavy flooding. *Glowworm* sank with the loss of over a hundred lives.

search was carried out. Then, just before 0800hrs on 8 April, while 50 miles west of Trondheim, *Glowworm* encountered the German heavy cruiser *Admiral Hipper* emerging through the fog accompanied by two destroyers. In the singularly unequal contest that followed, Roope's destroyer was sunk, but not before having launched torpedoes at *Hipper*, and then ramming the enemy cruiser. Roope was posthumously awarded the Victoria Cross – the first Royal Naval recipient of the war. However, 109 of his crew also died in the action. This clash, though, warned Forbes that the enemy were nearby.

In response, Forbes ordered *Repulse* and *Penelope* to go to *Glowworm*'s assistance, even though it was just to search for survivors, while Whitworth in *Renown* with the nine remaining destroyers was to cruise inshore, to cut off the enemy if they headed north. At 1430hrs a floatplane spotted a German force at sea off Trondheim. It was *Hipper* and her escorting destroyers. The redeployment south therefore continued, but this diversion had two unfortunate consequences. The first was that it left Narvik unguarded, and the following day, Tuesday 9 April, German forces landed there, screened by ten destroyers. The second was that early on 9 April, as the British battlecruisers were conducting a sweep to the east of the Lofoten Islands, *Renown* encountered the German battleships *Scharnhorst* and *Gneisenau*, off the entrance to the Vestfjord, the channel between the Lofoten Islands and the Norwegian mainland which led to Narvik.

Having failed to make any contact with the enemy when heading south, Whitworth turned north again, and early on 9 April he encountered *Scharnhorst* and *Gneisenau* south-west of the Lofoten Islands. In the brief duel that followed, both sides were hampered by the rough seas and stormy weather, but *Renown* had the better of the encounter, damaging both German battleships. While *Renown* was unhurt from this encounter, light damage was suffered due to the weather. Forbes and Whitworth took solace in the fact that they had bested the Kriegsmarine's two capital ships. The hope remained that Forbes himself could still bring them to battle with *Rodney* and *Valiant*. However, it also meant that Whitworth was unable to intervene in Narvik, and the German landing went ahead without British interference. In fact, so too did all six of the German landings, from Narvik to Oslo.

THE HOME FLEET OFF NORWAY, 8 APRIL 1940 (overleaf)

Following reports of the planned German invasion of Norway, the main body of the Home Fleet left Scapa Flow and put to sea. Dawn on Monday 8 April saw them 100 miles to the west of Bergen, cruising northwards, parallel to the Norwegian coast. As Admiral Forbes was unsure of the situation in Norway, he kept clear of her territorial waters until things became clearer. That morning, Forbes' battle fleet was made up of the battleships *Rodney* and *Valiant*, which were screened by light cruisers and destroyers. Other forces under his deputy, Vice-Admiral Whitworth were also at sea, 300 miles ahead of him. Both groups were searching for any sign of the German Kriegsmarine.

Shortly before 0900hrs one of Whitworth's destroyers, HMS *Glowworm*, encountered the German heavy cruiser *Admiral Hipper*. *Glowworm* was sunk, and so Forbes detached forces to hunt down the German heavy cruiser, last seen to the west of Trondheim. Forbes' ship continued, steaming parallel to the coast, and he launched floatplanes from his battleships, to scout ahead of the fleet. The hope was to catch elements of the Kriegsmarine between the two British pincers. In the end though, Forbes never made contact, although early the following morning Whitworth would, off the Lofoten Islands. If Admiral Forbes had located the main German force – the battleships *Gneisenau* and *Scharnhorst* – given the firepower at his disposal, his chances of destroying the enemy ships would have been high.

This illustration shows Forbes' main force that afternoon as it cruised slowly towards the north-east, out of sight of the coast. By this stage the weather had deteriorated, and a gale was brewing. Still, they continued, in the hope of intercepting the *Admiral Hipper*. Here, Admiral Forbes' flagship *Rodney* is in the foreground, the Admiral's flag flying from the battleship's foremast. Her Swordfish floatplane can be seen atop the catapult mounted on the roof of 'X' turret. Behind the aircraft, hanging off the port side of the battleship's superstructure, is the crane used for aircraft handling. The unusual layout of the battleship is clearly visible, with her nine powerful 16in guns mounted in three triple turrets, all emplaced forward of her superstructure. While she appeared ungainly, and lacked the speed of more modern battleship, *Rodney*'s firepower was second to none.

The Queen Elizabeth-class battleship HMS *Valiant* is shown following astern of the flagship. Both battleships, at this stage of the war, were painted in mid grey overall, with unpainted wooden decks. *Valiant*, who had seen action at Jutland, carried eight 15in guns, mounted in four twin turrets. She too carried a Swordfish floatplane – in fact two of them with their catapult fitted amidships, just behind the aircraft's hangar. Off *Rodney*'s port beam is a destroyer – one of a pair on station on either beam of the battleships. Out of sight, ahead of the flagship, was a cruiser screen, made up of the light cruisers *Galatea*, *Arethusa*, *Sheffield* and the French *Emile Bertin*. Farther ahead, out of sight was a destroyer screen.

Both *Rodney* and *Valiant* were fitted with Type 79Y air search radars, which were primitive, but better than nothing. The main threat though, at this opening stage of the Norwegian campaign, was German surface warships rather than aircraft. That day, if Admiral Forbes had made contact with the enemy battleship force, then the course of the naval campaign might have been markedly different. Instead, no contact was made, and the opportunity passed. Still, this artwork captures something of the power and the majesty of these great battleships, at a time when they still exerted an influence on the outcome of the naval war. *Rodney*'s time would come though, just over a year later, when she helped sink the German battleship *Bismarck*.

While Forbes remained at sea off the Norwegian coast, with his main force remaining outside Norwegian waters, he planned to send his light cruisers to attack any German forces off Bergen that afternoon, but at the last minute the Admiralty stayed his hand. Instead the fleet came under air attack as it cruised north up the Norwegian coast, and the destroyer *Gurkha* was sunk. This encouraged the Admiralty to keep out of southern Norwegian waters, and so rely on submarines and aircraft to challenge the Germans there. In the end, Forbes decided to launch his strike against Narvik. Before dawn on 9 April, due to the rough weather, Whitworth had detached his accompanying destroyers, and they were now guarding the entrance to the Vestfjord. Now they would be let loose.

At 1600hrs Captain Warburton-Lee, commanding the destroyer flotilla, had learned that there were up to six German destroyers off Narvik. He proposed attacking at high water, around dawn the following morning. Both Forbes and the Admiralty approved of the plan, therefore at 0430hrs on Wednesday 10 April, Warburton-Lee led his five destroyers into the fjord. In the hard-fought battle that followed the Germans were surprised, losing two destroyers off the port, while three more were damaged. Three more German destroyers were farther up the fjord, and when these arrived Warburton-Lee withdrew. In the pursuit that followed, the destroyers *Hardy* and *Hunter* were lost, and Warburton-Lee was killed. It was a costly victory for the British, but it made Forbes and Whitworth even more determined to deal with the remaining destroyers. For the moment, they had to be content with blockading them in the fjord.

For the next two days Forbes was fully occupied dealing with Admiralty interference, in a sequence of contradictory orders that ultimately led to the Home Fleet's temporary inaction. Forbes planned to launch an air strike on German warships off Trondheim using 18 torpedo bombers flying from *Furious*. However, this was delayed so long that their primary target, the *Admiral Hipper* and four attached destroyers, slipped away to the south, and the cruiser evaded the British in the course of limping home for repairs. The air strike, when it came at dawn on Thursday 11 April, found the Trondheimfjord all but deserted. The three German destroyers remaining there avoided damage as the water proved too shallow for the British aerial torpedoes to work properly. The Germans then launched air attacks of their own, which continued throughout the day.

In the meantime, Lütjens with *Scharnhorst* and *Gneisenau* also slipped past Forbes' fleet by keeping well out to sea. Around noon on 11 April they were spotted off the south-western tip of Norway, in company with the *Admiral Hipper*. A large-scale RAF bomber force was sent to intercept them, but the German ships were hidden by rain and sleet, reaching Wilhelmshaven without incident the following evening. It was a real blow for Forbes, as bringing them to battle would have restored British fortunes in the campaign. The only German force of any note within reach were the destroyers off Narvik. During Friday

12 April Forbes led the Home Fleet north, and that afternoon he took up position off the Lofoten Islands, in support of Whitworth. Plans were then drawn up for a return to Narvik – this time in force.

Early on 13 April, Forbes ordered Whitworth to send the newly arrived battleship *Warspite* into the fjord, accompanied by nine destroyers. Low clouds and bad weather prevented any air support from *Furious*, but at 1230hrs on Saturday 13 April *Warspite* entered the Ofotfjord which led to Narvik. Captain Crutchley ordered *Warspite*'s Swordfish floatplane to be launched, which duly spotted and bombed a U-boat, *U-64*, which was sunk. As *Warspite* and the destroyers worked their way up the fjord they sank three German destroyers and forced five more to scuttle. The only serious damage to the British force was inflicted on the destroyer *Eskimo*, her bow being blown off by a torpedo. However, *Eskimo* eventually reached Britain and was repaired. This action, the Second Battle of Narvik, was a complete success for the British. In the two Narvik battles, over the space of three days, the Kriegsmarine had lost half of its entire operational destroyer fleet.

This was only the start. The German amphibious force had already landed at Narvik, and there, as elsewhere in Norway, they were able to consolidate their bridgehead and then drive back the Norwegian defenders. For the Home Fleet this ushered in a new phase of the campaign. It had been unsuccessful in preventing the German landings, and in intercepting the various Kriegsmarine groups which had supported them, so, after Narvik, the emphasis became the denial of these waters to the Germans, who were desperate to reinforce and supply their troops, and in the safe transport of Allied troops to Norway to assist the Norwegians. On 10 April Admiral of the Fleet William Boyle, Earl of Cork was named as Flag Officer, Narvik, flying his flag in the light cruiser *Aurora*. From 14 April he was based in the Skjelfjord in the Lofoten Islands, and Forbes detached *Warspite* and *Furious* plus other lighter forces to operate under his command.

From this point on, Forbes had to liaise with Lord Cork as well as the Admiralty, while his fleet operated in Norwegian waters. This inevitably led to some confusion. Over the following two months the Home Fleet was involved in a succession of operations, each designed to support the land campaign in Norway. This began on 11 April, when the first British troop transports bound for Norway left the Clyde, and continued until the final Allied evacuation of Norway on 10 June. On 21 April, Lord Cork became the overall Allied commander in Norway, and oversaw the deployment of Allied troops to Namsos and Åndalsnes, to encircle the Germans at Trondheim. Eventually, a combination of heavy German bombing and the advance of German forces northwards from Lillehammer led to an evacuation of these troops by Forbes' light cruisers and destroyers.

Inevitably, the Home Fleet had to support these troop movements, while maintaining a close blockade of Narvik. As these events were unfolding during

The new Illustrious-class fleet carrier *Victorious* joined the Home Fleet in mid-April 1941, but the crew were still undergoing training when *Victorious* accompanied the fleet during its pursuit of the German battleship *Bismarck*, as no other carrier was available. Despite this, on 24 May *Victorious*'s raw pilots carried out a nighttime air strike on the German battleship.

late April and early May, the Admiralty steadily reduced the strength of Forbes' command, redeploying several of his ships to the Mediterranean in response to growing Italian hostility. These included *Warspite*, which left Narvik on 24 April. Five days later the light cruiser *Glasgow* and two destroyers put in to Molde near Åndalsnes, to evacuate the Norwegian king and crown prince, and the country's gold reserves. They were evacuated from the burning town amid a heavy air attack. The evacuation of troops from Åndalsnes and Namsos was also carried out in the face of near-constant air attacks.

Vice Admiral Edward-Collins commanding the 18th Cruiser Squadron took *Galatea*, *Arethusa*, *Sheffield*, *Southampton* and six destroyers into Åndalsnes on the night of 30/31 April, and took off 2,200 men without incident. However, on 1–3 May, when Vice Admiral Cunningham's 1st Cruiser Squadron tried a similar operation, it was less straightforward. Thick fog meant that the cruisers *Devonshire*, *York* and the French *Montcalm* had to remain offshore, and it was left to the destroyers to spearhead the evacuation. They led in the handful of transports and began embarking troops. However, the operation took time, and after dawn the fog cleared sufficiently for the Luftwaffe to discover what was happening. From noon on, both the destroyers and Cunningham's cruisers were subjected to a series of heavy attacks by Stuka dive bombers. Despite the loss of the destroyer *Afridi* and the French destroyer *Bison*, the evacuation was successful and 5,400 Allied troops were brought to safety.

The only remaining concentration of Allied troops was in the vicinity of Narvik. Here, both naval and land operations were under the control of Lord Cork. It was clear that the turning point in the campaign had been passed. With the airfields of central and southern Norway in German hands, the Luftwaffe was able to dominate the skies over Narvik, and so threaten any naval operations envisaged by either Cork or Forbes. However, on 10 May the Germans invaded France and the Low Countries, and overnight Norway became something of a sideshow. The Home Fleet, though, was fully committed to the Norway campaign, which still involved denying Norwegian waters to the Germans and supporting Allied land forces. Just over a week later the light cruiser *Effingham*, the new flagship of Lord Cork, ran aground near Bødo, 80 miles south of Narvik, and had to be abandoned. Then, on 26 May, the anti-aircraft cruiser *Curlew* was sunk in an air attack off Harstad, to the north of Narvik. The Narvik operation was becoming increasingly costly. However, worse was to come.

On 27 May, the Allies finally entered Narvik, but it was a pyrrhic victory. It was clear by then that the French campaign was going extremely badly and, the previous day, the evacuation of Allied troops from Dunkirk had begun. It was now inevitable that Norway would have to be abandoned. A week earlier Lord Cork had requested air support, therefore the Home Fleet used the carriers *Furious* and *Glorious* to transport RAF fighters to Norway. However, it was too late to make a difference. On 1 June the decision was made to evacuate the 24,500 Allied troops in Narvik. Once again, it was the Home Fleet that provided the ships. *Ark Royal* and *Glorious* provided air cover for the evacuation, while Rear Admiral Vivian, commanding the Home Fleet's anti-aircraft ships, supervised the embarkation from the AA cruiser *Coventry*. The evacuation began in earnest on 4 June.

Lord Cork remained in overall command of the operation, with the cruisers *Coventry* and *Southampton* and the repair ship *Vindictive* under his direct command, plus ten destroyers. Within four days the evacuation was complete, and the troops reached the Clyde without incident. Nevertheless, elements of the Home Fleet were still in Norwegian waters after Lord Cork's force had sailed away to safety. It was unfortunate for Forbes that this coincided with a powerful German sortie into the Norwegian Sea. Codenamed Operation *Juno*, this was a robust sweep through Norwegian waters, climaxing in an attack on British naval forces around Narvik. It was led by Vizeadmiral Lütjens in *Gneisenau*, accompanied by *Scharnhorst*, the *Admiral Hipper* and four destroyers. However, he had no idea that the Allies were already withdrawing from Norway.

Lütjens slipped out of Kiel early on 4 June, and two days later he was in the Norwegian Sea, midway between the Faeroes and the Vestfjord. He cruised northwards, narrowly missing the Allied troop convoys. At 1600hrs on 8 June Lütjens came upon the carrier *Glorious*, escorted by two destroyers, *Acasta* and *Ardent*. *Glorious* was low on fuel, and heading back to Scapa Flow, with a flight deck full of RAF fighters. The Germans closed the range, and at 1630hrs, *Scharnhorst* opened fire at a range of 14 miles. The British destroyers tried to screen their charge with smoke, but it wasn't enough. *Scharnhorst*'s fire was accurate, and *Glorious* was hit with the third salvo, wrecking the flight deck and bridge, and killing the carrier's commander, Captain Oyly-Hughes. More hits followed, leaving the helpless carrier listing and on fire. At 1720hrs the order was given to abandon ship, and *Glorious* capsized and sank 20 minutes later. Only 43 of the crew survived to be rescued by Norwegian fishing boats.

Meanwhile, while *Acasta* remained with *Glorious*, laying smoke, *Ardent* charged towards *Scharnhorst*, trying to get within torpedo range. *Ardent* managed to launch a salvo, but moments later the destroyer was torn apart by *Scharnhorst*'s guns. *Ardent*'s torpedoes missed, but *Acasta* was marginally more fortunate. Using a smokescreen as cover Commander Glasfurd of *Acasta* launched four torpedoes, one of which struck *Scharnhorst* below the after turret. It was a serious blow. However, when Glasfurd tried to close the range to launch a second torpedo attack, *Acasta* was hit and brought to a stop. The torpedoes

Admiral Sir Charles Forbes (1880–1960), Commander-in-Chief of the Home Fleet during the first year of the war. He had seen action aboard the fleet flagship *Iron Duke* at Jutland (1916) and had a distinguished inter-war career, culminating in his appointment as the Home Fleet's commander in 1938.

were fired, but they missed their target. *Acasta* sank with guns still firing at the battleship. Only one of the crew lived to tell the tale, along with two more survivors from *Ardent*. It was a costly day for the Royal Navy, but Lütjens hadn't emerged unscathed. As a result, he ordered his force to reverse course and head for Trondheim for emergency repairs. This probably saved the troop convoys, which were just over the horizon to the north.

Leaving *Glorious* so poorly protected was a grave mistake, but Forbes had had no choice. Reports of German raiders in the Iceland–Faeroes gap had led the Admiralty to order Forbes to hunt for them there. Consequently, when *Glorious* was attacked, Forbes with *Rodney* was still in Scapa Flow, awaiting news, while Whitworth with *Repulse* and *Renown* were out searching for the non-existent raider. Forbes sped north, with *Renown* in company, while the battleship *Valiant* was sent to protect the troop convoys. By then, Lütjens had reached Trondheim. Meanwhile both *Valiant* and the carrier *Ark Royal* were spotted by the Luftwaffe and subjected to air attacks, but were unscathed. The convoys they were escorting reached the Clyde without incident. Lütjens made another brief sortie on 10 June, leaving the damaged *Scharnhorst* behind, but turned back as the Luftwaffe reported that no enemy forces were within range.

This effectively brought the Norwegian campaign to an end. Overall, the performance of the Home Fleet had been exemplary – the attacks on Narvik had been well executed, as had the operations involving the landing and then evacuation of Allied troops. However, as the loss of *Glorious* and the two escorts showed, there was poor coordination between fleet operations and convoy movement and the RAF, who had failed to provide the air reconnaissance Forbes needed. If they had, *Glorious*, *Ardent* and *Acasta* would probably have survived. Instead, Lütjens' Operation *Juno* had taken Forbes and his commanders completely by surprise. It was unfortunate that Forbes had been unable to locate and engage the two German battleships during Operation *Weserübung*. The brief clash between *Renown* and the two German battleships on 9 April had been too short to allow Forbes and Whitworth to bring about a decisive clash. If they had, the course of the naval war might well have taken a markedly different course.

The Atlantic Raiders

The Home Fleet had little time to regroup in the wake of the Norwegian campaign. By then, the southern portion of the North Sea and the English Channel had been allocated to independent commands, and it was these that bore the brunt of Operation *Dynamo*, the evacuation of Allied troops from Dunkirk and other nearby ports. Similarly, Admiral Forbes had no direct involvement in the growing cross-Channel struggle between British and German light forces. At the same time, Plymouth Command had assumed responsibility for convoy operations in the Western Approaches, the Atlantic waters immediately to the west of the British Isles. By late 1940 this had evolved into the Western Approaches Command, based in Liverpool. This allowed the Home Fleet to concentrate on its primary responsibility – denying the surface arm of the Kriegsmarine access to the Atlantic. Nevertheless, it remained in readiness should the Germans attempt an invasion of southern England.

This threat also led to the Home Fleet being stripped of many of its destroyers, at a time when Forbes was fully occupied re-establishing his blockade lines from Greenland to the Faeroes, by way of Iceland, and from there to the Scottish mainland. Larger warships were also frequently detached from Forbes' command and sent to other theatres, most notably the Mediterranean, where the need for them was considered more pressing. Forbes simply had to make do with whatever forces he had left. His only good fortune was that *Scharnhorst* was still undergoing repairs, and while the new German battleship *Bismarck* was now in commission, it would be some time before this opponent was ready for active service. However, that still left the Kriegsmarine's cruisers and armed merchant raiders.

By October 1940 the Germans had six of these disguised merchantmen at sea, but apart from preventing their passage of the blockade line, there was little the Home Fleet could do about them. A more immediate threat was posed by the heavy cruiser *Admiral Hipper* and the armoured cruiser *Admiral Scheer*. Intelligence reports suggested both were earmarked for commerce-raiding voyages in the Atlantic, as were *Scharnhorst* and *Gneisenau* when they finished repairing the damage they had sustained off Norway. The Home Fleet had already experienced the challenges facing the interception of Atlantic raiders. When hostilities began in September 1939, the armoured cruiser *Deutschland* was already in the North Atlantic, and hunted there for the next two months before returning undetected by way of the Denmark Strait. Bad weather helped the cruiser's passage through the British patrols off Norway, and *Deutschland* arrived safely in Gotenhafen on 15 November.

Six days later *Scharnhorst* and *Gneisenau* sailed from Wilhelmshaven and headed north, passing through the Northern Patrol in bad weather without being detected. On 23 November, when they entered the Faeroes gap between the Faeroes and Iceland, they encountered the armed merchant cruiser *Rawalpindi*. The merchant cruiser was sunk by gunfire from the battleships, but the German force commander, Vizeadmiral Marschall, then withdrew into the Norwegian Sea. At the time, only light cruisers lay between his two battleships and the Atlantic, and the delay bought time for Admiral Forbes to reinforce his blockading force with *Rodney* and *Nelson*. Although the German force then returned to Wilhelmshaven without incident – again using bad weather to screen its passage – the whole incident highlighted weaknesses in the British blockade. As a result, air patrols off southern Norway and the North Sea were stepped up, the Northern Patrol was strengthened, and Forbes tried to improve the response time of his capital ships by demanding a speedy improvement of Scapa Flow's defences, so he could return there rather than use the more southerly base of Loch Ewe.

On 23 October 1940 the *Admiral Scheer* left Gotenhafen, reaching Stavanger six days later where fuel was taken on board. *Admiral Scheer* then made the passage through the Denmark Strait in early November without being detected, and entered the North Atlantic. After sinking eight merchantmen there, *Admiral Scheer* moved on into the South Atlantic, and continued onwards.

THE BACKSTOP DEFENCE: BLOCKING ACCESS TO THE ATLANTIC 1939–41

After the Germans overran Norway, the Northern Patrol was withdrawn from Norwegian waters. In November 1940 it was broken up, save for a small presence in the Faeroes gap and the Denmark Strait, made up primarily of armed trawlers. By then the need to maintain a mercantile blockade had ended, as German blockade-running attempts had virtually ceased. So it fell to the Home Fleet to maintain a presence in the passages into the Atlantic Ocean, from Greenland to Orkney.

It was helped by the establishment of local bases. In April 1940, in reaction to the German invasion of Denmark, the British peaceably occupied the Faeroes. It was then used as a sheltered haven and a refuelling station for Allied warships. Even more significantly, in May 1940 the British conducted an equally peaceful invasion of Iceland, to prevent it from falling into German hands.

A useful by-product was that it provided the Home Fleet with a number of naval bases and refuelling stations. This allowed the patrol lines to be maintained much more easily. In addition, RAF and Fleet Air Arm airfields were established in Iceland, allowing maritime reconnaissance patrols to be flown above the Arctic Circle. Similarly, bases in Orkney, Shetland and Caithness were used to support the Home Fleet's operations, and to conduct reconnaissance flights over the Norwegian Sea and the coast of occupied Norway.

Cruisers were used to maintain the Home Fleet's patrols in the Denmark Strait, the Faeroes gap and the Faeroes to Shetland gap. By this stage, a presence in the Fair Isle Channel was largely left to smaller vessels, and air reconnaissance patrols. Each time naval intelligence warned that a German breakout attempt was imminent, a Supporting Force was sent from Scapa Flow to take up a waiting position to the south of Iceland. It usually consisted of the warships of the battlecruiser squadron, commanded by the Vice Admiral, Battlecruiser Squadron, and Second in Command, Home Fleet. It was then able to intercept any German attempt to penetrate the patrol lines and reach the Atlantic.

If contact was made, or was deemed imminent, the Commander-in-Chief, Home Fleet would sortie from Scapa Flow with the bulk of his battle fleet. He would then take up a position in the north Atlantic, where he could either reinforce his deputy's Supporting Force, or in the event the enemy bypassed the Supporting Force, it would attempt to pursue the enemy. All movements were closely monitored by the fleet commander in his flagship.

GREENLAND

Pack Ice
(summer)

Denmark Strait

Arctic Ocean

Arctic Circle

Arctic Circle

Atlantic Ocean

Ísafjörð (refuelling
station only)

Hvalfjörður

Reykjavik

RAF
Reykjavik

Akureyri

ICELAND

RAF Kaldadarnes

Seydisfjörður

Support Force
(holding position)

Norwegian Sea

Home Fleet

Faeroes

Tórshavn

Outer
Hebrides

Scapa
Flow

Shetland

RAF Wick

NAS Hatston, RAF Skeabrae

RAF Sumburgh

SCOTLAND

North Sea

NORWAY

Ålesund

Bergen

Stavanger

Refuelling station
Mines
Airfields
Harbour facilities

N
W · E
S

The armoured cruiser finally returned to Kiel on 1 April 1941, again without being intercepted by the Home Fleet. Similarly, the *Admiral Hipper* broke out into the Atlantic using the same passage on 7–8 December and cruised there for a month, before returning to Brest on 27 December. The only British warship *Admiral Hipper* encountered during all that time was the heavy cruiser *Berwick*, which formed part of the escort of Convoy WS5A. The *Hipper* fought a brief duel with *Berwick*, before abandoning the attack on the convoy.

This demonstrated that the Home Fleet still had serious problems maintaining an adequate blockade in the Denmark Strait. The only slight piece of good news for Admiral Tovey, the new Commander-in-Chief of the Home Fleet, was that this problem was recognized by the Admiralty, resulting in more cruisers being placed under Tovey's command. Nevertheless, these problems remained. On 22 January 1941, *Scharnhorst* and *Gneisenau* began their Atlantic sortie, codenamed Operation *Berlin*, under the command of Vizeadmiral Lütjens, who flew his flag in *Gneisenau*. Six days later Lütjens attempted a dawn passage through the Iceland–Faeroes gap, but turned back when he encountered the anti-aircraft cruiser *Naiad*. Lütjens withdrew, fearing this was the leading ship of a much larger British force. He had more luck passing through the Denmark Strait on 4 February, which he managed without being detected.

In both cases Lütjens had been lucky. Tovey had stationed the battlecruiser *Repulse* and four destroyers off Iceland, ready to respond to any attempted German breakout. On 28 January Lütjens had withdrawn before *Renown* could intervene, and a week later the battlecruiser was refuelling when Lütjens slipped through the Denmark Strait. Tovey was also at sea with *Nelson* and *Rodney* in late January, and the cruiser patrols in all passages through into the Atlantic were strong enough to guarantee a sighting of the enemy should they appear.

Lütjens conveniently sidestepped the Home Fleet by remaining in the Arctic Sea until the British ships had to return home to refuel. Then, with the help of bad weather and poor visibility, he was able to reach the Atlantic without being challenged. After a successful cruise, the two German battleships reached Brest safely on 22 March, after sinking or capturing 22 Allied merchant ships. Two days later, on 24 March *Admiral Hipper* returned home to Germany by way of

The second King George V-class battleship to join the Home Fleet was *Prince of Wales* in April 1941. The battleship is pictured here off the coast of Orkney when still undergoing 'snagging work' on the main guns and turrets. Despite this, *Prince of Wales* accompanied *Hood* in an attempt to stop the German battleship *Bismarck*. *Hood* was sunk, and *Prince of Wales* damaged in the resulting engagement on 24 May 1941, but the British battleship scored two hits on *Bismarck*.

the Denmark Strait. Once again the heavy cruiser's passage went undetected and *Hipper* reached Kiel without incident four days later.

The Admiralty's response to these successful German sorties was to deploy slower battleships and some heavy cruisers as escorts to important transatlantic or Sierra Leone convoys. This inevitably meant that the strength of the Home Fleet was reduced at a critical time in the naval campaign. The only positive for Tovey was that it seemed the Germans were unwilling to press home a breakout if they discovered their passage through the British patrol lines was detected.

The *Bismarck* Sortie

Operation *Rheinübung*, the German codename for the sortie of the brand-new battleship *Bismarck*, began a little after noon on 18 May 1941. *Bismarck* put to sea from Gotenhafen, accompanied by the heavy cruiser *Prinz Eugen*. Once again the force was commanded by Vizeadmiral Lütjens. After rendezvousing with a destroyer screen the two ships continued on to the Kattegat, where at 1300hrs on 20 May their passage was sighted by the neutral Swedish cruiser *Gotland*. The British were told of the sighting, which was then confirmed by the Norwegian resistance, as the German warships passed Kristiansand. At 1315 the following day, *Bismarck* was spotted again, this time taking on fuel in the Grimstadfjord, just south of Bergen. In response, Tovey ordered his deputy Vice Admiral Holland to put to sea from Scapa Flow with the battlecruiser *Hood* and the battleship *Prince of Wales*, accompanied by six destroyers. Holland's task was to wait to the south of Iceland, ready to intercept *Bismarck* if the battleship attempted to pass through the Denmark Strait or the Iceland–Faeroes gap.

Early on the morning of Thursday 22 May an RAF bombing raid on the Grimstadfjord revealed that the Germans had already departed. Tovey deployed his forces accordingly. The usual patrol line in the Iceland–Faeroes gap of five armed trawlers was reinforced by the light cruisers *Arethusa*, *Manchester* and *Birmingham*. The heavy cruisers *Norfolk* and *Suffolk* were ordered to patrol the Denmark Strait. Finally, at 2300hrs, Tovey sailed from Scapa Flow in his flagship *King George V*, accompanied by the fleet carrier *Victorious*, the light cruisers *Aurora*, *Galatea* and *Kenya*, the AA cruiser *Hermione* and seven destroyers. Off the Western Isles he was joined by the battlecruiser *Repulse*, which had steamed north from the Clyde. Tovey planned to remain well to the south of Iceland, forming a second tier of defence, if Holland failed to intercept Lütjens. In addition air patrols were stepped up from bases in Orkney and Shetland, and also Iceland.

Lütjens opted to break out through the Denmark Strait. After detaching his destroyers off the Norwegian coast, *Bismarck* and *Prinz Eugen* continued on around the north of Norway, their progress screened by fog. On the early evening of Friday 23 May they approached the Denmark Strait. At 1922hrs *Suffolk* sighted *Bismarck*, as the Germans pressed on through the Strait, and the two British cruisers shadowed the Germans throughout the night, sending regular sighting

COORDINATED ACTION: THE HUNT FOR THE *BISMARCK*, MAY 1941

Operation *Rheinübung*, the sortie of the German battleship *Bismarck* represented a particular challenge for Admiral Tovey. *Bismarck* was faster than his two most powerful battleships, and was more than a match for any other capital ship in the Home Fleet. To counter her, Tovey needed good intelligence – a forewarning of her breakout attempt – and he needed to deploy his forces with precision. He also needed a fair amount of luck.

Vizeadmiral Lütjens in the battleship *Bismarck*, accompanied by the heavy cruiser *Prinz Eugen*, had three routes into the North Atlantic. After leaving the Norwegian coast late on Wed 21 May, he opts for the Denmark Strait. On patrol in this channel is Rear Admiral Wake-Walker with the heavy cruisers *Suffolk* and *Norfolk*. The Faeroes Gap is patrolled by Captain Madden with the light cruisers *Arethusa*, *Manchester* and *Birmingham*.

Phase 1 Atlantic Breakout (22–23 May)

1. At 0015hrs on Thu 22 May, on Tovey's orders, Vice Admiral Holland sailed from Scapa Flow in the battlecruiser *Hood*, accompanied by the battleship *Prince of Wales* and a destroyer escort. His orders were to take up position to the south of Iceland, and await developments.

2. At 2300hrs that evening, Tovey left Scapa Flow in the battleship *King George V*, accompanied by the Fleet carrier *Victorious*, the light cruisers *Aurora*, *Galatea*, *Kenya* and *Neptune*, and six destroyers. Early the following morning, he was joined by the battlecruiser *Repulse*.

3. At 1800hrs on Fri 23 May, Lütjens entered the Denmark Strait. He was sighted by *Suffolk* and *Norfolk* at 19.22hrs, and was shadowed through the evening.

4. Tovey ordered Holland to intercept the German force at around dawn the following morning,

Phase 2 Battle and Pursuit (24–25 May)

5. In the Battle of the Denmark Strait (0537hrs–0609hrs Sat, 24 May), *Hood* was sunk, with all but three of her crew lost, including Vice Admiral Holland. *Prince of Wales* was damaged and broke off the action.

6. Lütjens headed south, shadowed by Wake-Walker's cruisers, and by *Prince of Wales*. Damage to *Bismarck* forced Lütjens' hand, and he decided to abort the operation and head to Brest on the French Atlantic coast for repairs.

7. Tovey set a course to intercept *Bismarck*, guided by sighting reports from Wake-Walker's cruisers. His aim was to launch an air strike from *Victorious* when the carrier moved within range.

8. The Admiralty detached the battleship *Rodney* from convoy-escort duties, and ordered her to reinforce Tovey. Similarly five destroyers under Captain Vian were also detached from escort duties, and were ordered to join Tovey's battle fleet.

9. At 1815hrs, Lütjens successfully detached *Prinz Eugen*, which began an independent cruise in the North Atlantic.

10. At 1830hrs, Tovey detached *Victorious* and his cruisers to close the gap with *Bismarck*. He continued on with *King George V* and *Repulse*, on a course designed to intercept *Bismarck* at dawn.

11. At 0015hrs on Sun 25 May, *Bismarck* was attacked by Swordfish torpedo bombers launched from *Victorious*. She suffered a hit amidships, but no significant damage was caused.

12. At 0315hrs, *Bismarck* managed to evade Wake-Walker's shadowing cruisers. By dawn, as Tovey reached the area, there was no sign of the German battleship. Having been thwarted in his attempts to bring *Bismarck* to battle, Tovey began an ocean-wide search for the German battleship.

Bismarck was eventually spotted early on Mon 26 May, and Tovey pursued her. His chance of intercepting *Bismarck* was slim, but Vice Admiral Somerville's Force H approaching from the south was better placed. At 2100hrs, *Bismarck* was damaged in an attack by Swordfish torpedo bombers flying from *Ark Royal*. *Bismarck*'s rudder was damaged, which allowed Tovey to overhaul during the night. At 0845hrs on Tue 27 May, *King George V* and *Rodney* engaged *Bismarck* in a climactic final battle. The German battleship sank at 1040hrs, taking all but 116 of her crew with her, including Vizeadmiral Lütjens. With that, Tovey ordered the Home Fleet to return to Scapa Flow.

reports back to Tovey. At this stage Holland was off the south-east of Iceland, and although he had sent his destroyers off to Reykjavik to refuel, he pressed on, to block the exit from the Strait into the Atlantic. At 0537hrs the following morning, Saturday 24 May, the two forces sighted each other at a range of 17 miles.

At 0552hrs, Holland ordered his ships to open fire. Surprisingly, *Prinz Eugen* was ahead of *Bismarck*, and mistakenly *Hood* engaged the heavy cruiser. Captain Leach of *Prince of Wales* recognized that the second ship was *Bismarck*, and targeted the battleship instead. Initially, due to the angle of the two forces, only the front turrets of the British ships could bear on the enemy. Holland was keen to decrease the range as, due to having thin deck armour, *Hood* was more vulnerable at long range, as shells would plunge down vertically rather than on a flatter trajectory which would hit the battlecruiser's well-protected hull. At 0554, Lütjens turned to starboard in an attempt to 'cross the T' of the British – ensuring all his guns could fire on the enemy, while only the front British guns could respond. A minute later Holland ordered his two capital ships to turn to port too, so all his guns could bear.

Having got the range of *Hood*, at 0559hrs *Bismarck* fired three salvoes at *Hood* in quick succession. A minute later, at 0600hrs, one of *Bismarck*'s 15in shells struck the after deck of *Hood*, close to the after gun turrets, and the shell detonated, which in turn detonated the charges in *Hood*'s after magazine. The resulting explosion sent up an immense plume of fire, and the stern was blown off the battlecruiser. *Hood* sank quickly, taking all but three of the crew down too. Farther astern, the stunned commander of *Prince of Wales* skirted around the wreckage of the British flagship and continued the fight. However, *Bismarck*'s guns turned on *Prince of Wales*, and at 0604 the battleship sustained a direct hit to the bridge, injuring Leach and killing most of his bridge crew. Another shell from *Prinz Eugen* knocked out the British battleship's secondary gunnery director. The battleship's 14in guns were also malfunctioning, despite having inflicted two hits on *Bismarck*.

The sortie of the German battleship represented the Home Fleet's greatest challenge during this period. *Bismarck* was fast, well protected and well armed – the most modern battleship in existence. Admiral Tovey brought this adversary to bay, by a combination of skill, foresight and a large slice of luck.

At 0605hrs, when it was reported 'X' turret had jammed, Leach decided to break off the action. He contacted Rear Admiral Wake-Walker, commanding the two British cruisers which were still shadowing *Bismarck*, and this withdrawal was approved. Accordingly, at 0609hrs, *Prince of Wales* turned away, making smoke, and broke off the action. The Battle of the Denmark Strait had been a great triumph for Lütjens, but it had come at a price. The two hits on *Bismarck* caused flooding, and the loss of fuel; *Bismarck* was also down by the bow. As a result, Lütjens decided to abort Operation *Rheinübung* and instead head for Brest, in German-occupied France. However, he was still being shadowed by Wake-Walker's two cruisers and by the battered *Prince of Wales*. News of the loss of *Hood* sent shockwaves around the world, and stunned both the Royal Navy and the British public. During the inter-war years the graceful battlecruiser had become the epitome of British naval might.

After the initial shock had passed, Tovey and the men of the Home Fleet resolved to avenge *Hood* and the ship's crew by pursuing and sinking the *Bismarck*. At the time, Tovey's force was 300 miles away to the south-west of *Bismarck*, so Tovey pressed on, guided by regular sighting reports from Wake-Walker's cruisers. During the day, other ships were found to reinforce the Home Fleet's battle group. The battleship *Rodney* was detached from escort duty with a transatlantic troop convoy. The battleship *Ramillies* and a five-destroyer force under Captain Vian was also detached from Atlantic convoys and ordered to join Tovey. During the day Lütjens decided to detach *Prinz Eugen*, and at 1815hrs he succeeded, after *Bismarck* turned round to engage with the pursuers. Captain Brinkmann's cruiser then headed south, to commence an independent commerce-raiding cruise in the Atlantic.

By then Tovey was drawing closer to the *Bismarck*, and at 2300hrs, *Victorious* launched an air strike made up of nine Swordfish torpedo bombers. Their inexperienced air crews successfully found *Bismarck* and attacked the battleship, albeit without any success. One torpedo hit the battleship's starboard beam but

The battlecruiser *Hood* blowing up, as seen from the German heavy cruiser *Prinz Eugen* during the Battle of the Denmark Strait, soon after dawn on 24 May 1941. *Hood* was struck by the 6th salvo fired by *Bismarck*, and one shell detonated a magazine, blowing off the British battlecruiser's stern. All but three of the crew were lost.

caused no significant damage. The pursuit continued, and at 0131hrs on Sunday 25 May *Bismarck* turned again, this time to drive off *Prince of Wales*, which had come within gun range. No hits were scored by either ship, and *Bismarck* then resumed the run to the south. Almost two hours later Lütjens managed to evade his pursuers, and slip away under cover of darkness. The British now had no idea where *Bismarck* was. Tovey ordered all of his ships to search for the battleship, but by dawn it was clear that *Bismarck* had slipped clean away.

When dawn broke on Sunday 25 May, Tovey had no idea where *Bismarck* was. So, he was unable to deploy his fleet to intercept the enemy battleship. Early that morning *Prince of Wales* had to be detached to refuel, leaving Tovey with just *King George V* and *Repulse*. What complicated the situation was that there were still several convoys at sea in the Atlantic and any of them could be torn apart by the German battleship. Then word reached him that at 0930 that morning, Lütjens had sent a long radio report to Germany. As a result, British radio direction finders had discovered *Bismarck* was somewhere to the east of Tovey. Accordingly, Tovey turned east, while *Rodney* and the light cruiser *Edinburgh* to the south-east were ordered north to rendezvous with him. The day continued without any other clue as to where Lütjens was. It was a deeply worrying time for Tovey, but true to form the Home Fleet's commander didn't show it.

Finally, at 1030hrs on Monday 26 May, *Bismarck* was spotted by a Coastal Command Catalina aircraft some 500 miles from the southern tip of Ireland, and 690 miles from Brest. Tovey deployed his ships accordingly, but his flagship was 130 miles from the enemy and completely alone as *Repulse* had had to be detached to refuel. It was now almost certain that *Bismarck* was going to make it into Brest before the British could prevent it. Still the pursuit continued. Fortunately for Tovey, *Rodney* was able to join him at 1800hrs that evening, while Vice Admiral Somerville's Gibraltar-based Force H comprising the battlecruiser *Renown*, the fleet carrier *Ark Royal* and the light cruiser *Sheffield*, were heading up towards *Bismarck* from the south. At 1740hrs, *Sheffield* detected *Bismarck* on the ship's radar and began shadowing the battleship, as *Bismarck* headed at speed towards the French coast. Now Somerville had a chance to intervene.

The battleship *Bismarck* is brought to bay by the Home Fleet on 28 May 1941. That morning the crippled German battleship was engaged by *King George V* and *Rodney*, whose fire knocked out *Bismarck*'s guns. This photograph was taken from *Dorsetshire*, before the heavy cruiser was called on to deliver the *coup de grâce* with torpedoes.

Ark Royal had already attempted an air strike with 14 Swordfish, but had mistakenly attacked *Sheffield* rather than the German battleship being shadowed. Fortunately, problems with the torpedoes led to the cruiser emerging unscathed. The sheepish pilots returned to *Ark Royal*, their torpedoes were altered, and at 1910hrs a second wave of 15 Swordfish tried again. This time they located *Bismarck*, and began their attack. This was conducted in penny packets, over a space of 38 minutes. *Bismarck*'s Kapitän Lindemann did well to avoid most of them, but two of them struck *Bismarck*. One was an ineffective blow to the well-protected hull, but the second one struck the stern, damaging the propellers and jamming the rudders. As a result, *Bismarck*'s fate was sealed.

Unable to steer a straight course, and with a greatly reduced speed, *Bismarck* was now incapable of reaching Brest. That night, as the crew struggled to repair their ship, Vian's destroyers arrived and conducted a series of torpedo attacks. Although no hits were achieved, this forced *Bismarck*'s crew to remain at action stations throughout the night. It was clear that the situation was now hopeless, and Lütjens radioed the news to Germany. Meanwhile despite both ships being desperately short of fuel, *King George V* and *Rodney* were closing in on *Bismarck* from the west. Finally, at 0845hrs on Tuesday 27 May, they sighted *Bismarck*. Tovey gave the order to open fire two minutes later. At 0849hrs *Bismarck* returned fire, but due to the erratic steering the battleship's gunnery was inaccurate.

At 0859hrs, a 16in shell from *Rodney* hit *Bismarck*'s bridge, killing both Lütjens and Lindemann, and knocking out the German battleship's main gunnery director. Over the next 30 minutes, *Bismarck* was subjected to a relentless battering from the two British battleships, who gradually closed the range, to ensure greater accuracy. By 0930hrs, *Bismarck*'s guns had been silenced, and fierce fires raged on deck. Still the shells kept coming, being fired at what was effectively point-blank range. *Rodney* even launched a torpedo from the battleship's antiquated submerged torpedo tube. This hit was probably history's first occasion of one battleship torpedoing another. Shortly after 1015hrs, Tovey broke off the action, and the two battleships headed north to refuel.

It was left to the heavy cruiser *Dorsetshire* to finish *Bismarck* off with torpedoes. This was done at 1024hrs and 1030hrs, in two salvoes. By then, *Bismarck* was already sinking, as the crew had begun the process of scuttling the battleship. At 1040hrs, *Bismarck* finally sunk, leaving the survivors of the crew in the oil-slicked water. The recovery of the crew had to be broken off due to a U-boat threat, so in the end *Devonshire* and destroyer *Maori* recovered only 110 men, with six others being recovered later. That meant that over 1,800 of the crew were lost during *Bismarck*'s final battle. However, *Hood* had been avenged, and the Home Fleet's honour had been restored.

The sinking of *Bismarck* marked the end of the Kriegsmarine campaign of Atlantic raiding using surface ships. *Prinz Eugen* was the last of them, arriving safely in Brest on 1 June. From that point on the Battle of the Atlantic would be fought by the U-boat arm alone. This also ended the threat of a joint operation by the Kriegsmarine's powerful surface units. *Bismarck* was now lost, while *Scharnhorst* and *Gneisenau* were both damaged in air attacks on Brest and La Pallice near La Rochelle. The Kriegsmarine's surviving heavy cruisers and armoured cruisers were now scattered between Brest and Kiel, and so unable to form a concentrated force.

The whole strategic situation would change dramatically less than a month after *Bismarck's* loss. On 22 June, Operation *Barbarossa* began – the Axis invasion of the Soviet Union. Churchill immediately pledged Britain's support to Stalin, and three weeks later an Anglo–Soviet Agreement was signed. This assured Britain's support to the Soviets, and the United States weighed in, offering Lend Lease tanks, guns and aircraft. On 17 August, in what was codenamed Operation *Dervish*, a small convoy of six merchant ships and a tanker left Scapa Flow, bound for Archangel. The 'Dervish Convoy' would be the first of many Arctic Convoys, which would increase in size as the war progressed. From the start, the task of protecting these convoys fell to the Home Fleet and this would become the fleet's focus for the remainder of the war. The Germans, too, reacted to the commencement of these convoys by concentrating what remained of the Kriegsmarine's surface fleet in Norwegian waters. Accordingly, the war would enter a new phase, and the Home Fleet embarked on another long-running naval campaign, fought out in the icy wastes of the Arctic.

ANALYSIS

On 3 September 1939, when Britain found itself at war with Nazi Germany, the British Home Fleet was already prepared for the conflict. In effect, it followed a similar course of action as the British Grand Fleet had done in August 1914 – establishing a distant blockade of Germany, containing the German fleet and attempting to bring it to battle. The choice of Scapa Flow meant the fleet anchorage was beyond easy reach of German bombers, and after an initial disaster – the sinking of the battleship *Royal Oak* – the anchorage was rendered safe against attack by enemy U-boats, surface warships and even amphibious attack. So, its base secure, the fleet could set about waging its private war against the Kriegsmarine.

The strategic situation facing the Home Fleet changed dramatically in May 1940, when Germany invaded Denmark and Norway. This meant that the positioning of the Northern Patrol between Britain's North Isles and southern Norway was no longer practical. Therefore, it had to be moved north and west – a much longer cordon which eventually ran from Greenland to Shetland. For the next year, the primary job of the Home Fleet's Commander-in-Chief was to maintain this line of defence. It served both to enforce the distant blockade of Germany, much as the old Northern Patrol had, and also as a means of denying the Kriegsmarine's surface fleet access to the North Atlantic. Unfortunately, neither was as effective as the fleet commander had hoped.

It required a monumental effort to maintain this blockade. For instance, it was 875 miles from Scapa Flow to the patrol area in the Denmark Strait – the equivalent of a thousand land miles. Typically it would take a warship two days to make the journey between the two, therefore maintaining an effective patrol line took a monumental amount of planning, and was heavily reliant on the fleet maintaining a sufficient number of suitable warships to make the system work. This came at a time when the Royal Navy was badly over-stretched, particularly after Italy's entry into the war in mid-May 1940. Patrol work in these northern waters also inflicted a heavy toll on ships and men, as the weather conditions around the Arctic Circle were often extremely challenging. After spending time in those waters, ships frequently needed a period of refit and repair, and their crews needed time to recover from these extremely arduous deployments. As a result, the Home Fleet Commander was always hard-pressed to find the ships he needed to maintain an effective patrol line.

Although the German invasion of Norway took the Home Fleet unawares, Admiral Forbes had contingency plans in place to deal with the situation. This, of course, was partly because the British had already developed their own plan, Operation *Wilfred*, to intervene in Norwegian waters, in order to safeguard the transport of iron ore from Narvik. Forbes was unlucky during the Norwegian campaign, as thanks to poor intelligence gathering he wasn't able to intercept the German amphibious forces which were able to establish German footholds along the Norwegian coast, from Narvik down to Stavanger, then round to Oslo. This had less to do with Forbes' own dispositions, which were perfectly effective, but was more due to the lack of forewarning of Operation *Weserübung* from British intelligence sources.

During the campaign, the British sank ten German destroyers off Narvik and two light cruisers, one sunk by the Fleet Air Arm off Bergen and the other by a British submarine off Kristiansand. The Home Fleet's losses were also heavy, the most significant being the invaluable fleet carrier *Glorious*. In addition, the elderly light cruiser *Effingham* and the anti-aircraft cruiser *Curlew* were both lost, one due to running aground and the other in an air attack. Seven destroyers were sunk too, most through air attacks and two during the 1st Battle of Narvik. All in all the score sheet was even, apart from *Glorious*, whose loss was only counterpointed by the Norwegians' sinking of the German heavy cruiser *Blücher*

Today the remains of a number of blockships like this one can be seen next to the Churchill Barriers, which link four islands to the eastern side of the Orkney mainland. Before these four causeways were built, blockships were used to seal these four small channels leading into Scapa Flow.

in the Oslofjord. The loss of *Glorious* was a significant blow to the Royal Navy, but the carrier was quickly replaced by new fleet carriers under construction. For the Kriegsmarine, the warships sunk during the campaign represented a major and permanent reduction in the strength of Germany's operational fleet. The Home Fleet could absorb these losses – the Kriegsmarine could not.

More serious was the German acquisition of Norway as a base for its ships and aircraft. Now, Scapa Flow was within easy reach of German bombers, prompting a major effort to strengthen the anchorage's defences. The Northern Patrol line had to be abandoned, forcing the Home Fleet to impose its blockade over an arc from Greenland to the Scottish mainland which stretched for almost a thousand miles. The implications of this have already been discussed, but this, in conjunction with the availability of Norway as a forward base for Atlantic surface raiders as they prepared for their breakout, all conspired to increase the chances that a German breakout would be successful. The only way this could be effectively countered was by good intelligence gathering. If the Commander-in-Chief of the Home Fleet was forewarned of a breakout attempt, then he could deploy his forces accordingly.

Home Fleet operations were arguably more complex than those of many other naval commands during the opening years of World War II. Like operations in the Pacific theatre after December 1941, the need for intelligence, good planning and faultless fleet logistics were all of paramount importance in naval operations. It placed a heavy burden on the fleet commander and his small staff aboard his flagship, which, for much of the time, was moored in Scapa Flow, far from the corridors of the Admiralty in London. However, thanks to the establishment of a direct and secure phone link between the First Sea Lord's office and the flagship's mooring buoy off Flotta in Scapa Flow, this was no impediment to the flow of information, and other forms of support. As a result, while in Scapa Flow the Commander-in-Chief of the Home Fleet could draw on the staff of the Admiralty for advice, requests for logistical support, and above all the timely flow of intelligence information, including those all-important Ultra intercepts. Armed with this, the fleet commander had a much better chance of intercepting a German surface raider, if it tried to break through the British blockade.

The Home Fleet was Britain's naval guardian – her first line of defence against invasion, and also her best means of protection of the key Atlantic sea lanes, which were the lifeblood of wartime Britain. Despite all these challenges, and several major setbacks, the Home Fleet served Britain well during those dark years of war, when Britain fought on alone. Thanks to it, Britain survived those gruelling, challenging years. By the summer of 1941, when the Home Fleet acquired a new role and a fresh purpose, it would acquit itself equally well. In its support of the Arctic Convoys, and the final subjugation of the Kriegsmarine's surface fleet, it played a key part in the subjugation of Nazi Germany, and the securing of a decisive victory for the Allies.

FURTHER READING

Asmussen, John, *Bismarck: Pride of the German Navy* (Cirencester, Fonthill Media Ltd, 2013)

Brown, David K., *Nelson to Vanguard: Warship Design and Development, 1922–1945* (London, Chatham Publishing, 2003)

Campbell, John, *Naval Weapons of World War Two* (London, Conway Maritime Press, 1985)

Freidman, Norman, *Naval Radar* (London, Harper Collins, 1981)

Friedman, Norman, *Naval Firepower: Battleship Guns and Gunnery in the Dreadnought Era* (Barnsley, Seaforth Publishing, 2013)

Gardiner, Robert (ed.), *Conway's All the World's Fighting Ships* (London, Conway Maritime Press, 1980)

Gardiner, Robert (ed.), *The Eclipse of the Big Gun: The Warship, 1906–45*, Conway's History of the Ship Series (London, Conway Maritime Press, 1992)

Gröner, Erich, *German Warships, 1815–1945*, Vol. 1 *Major Surface Vessels* (London, Conway Maritime Press, 1983)

Heathcote, Tony, *The British Admirals of the Fleet 1734–1995* (Barnsley, Pen & Sword, 2002)

Hodges, Peter, *The Big Gun: Battleship Main Armament, 1860–1945* (London, Conway Maritime Press, 1981)

Jacobsen, Alf R., *Scharnhorst* (Stroud, Sutton Publishing, 2003)

Konstam, Angus, *Battleship Bismarck 1936–41, Owners' Workshop Manual* (Yeovil, Haynes Publishing, 2015)

Lavery, Brian, *Churchill's Navy: The Ships, Men and Organization, 1939–1945* (London, Conway Maritime Press, 2006)

Mallmann Showell, Jak P., *Hitler's Navy: A Reference Guide to the Kriegsmarine, 1939–45* (Barnsley, Seaforth Publishing, 2009)

Martienssen, Anthony, *Hitler and his Admirals* (New York, NY, Dutton Publishing, 1949)

Müllenheim-Rechberg, Burkard von, *Battleship Bismarck: A Survivor's Story* (Annapolis, MD, Naval Institute Press, 1990)

Parkes, Oscar, *British Battleships, 1860–1950: A History of Design, Construction and Armament* (London, Seeley Service & Co., 1966)

Roberts, John, *British Warships of the Second World War* (Barnsley, Seaforth Publishing, 2017)

Roskill, Stephen W., *The War at Sea*, Vols. 1 & 3, History of the Second World War Series (London HM Stationery Office, 1954)

Santarini, Marco, *Bismarck and Hood: The Battle of the Denmark Strait – A Technical Analysis for a New Perspective* (London, Fonthill Media, 2017)

Skwiot, Miroslaw Z. and Prusinowska, Elzbieta T., *Hunting the Bismarck* (Marlborough, Crowood Press, 2006)

Vulliez, Albert and Mordal, Jacques, *Battleship Scharnhorst* (London, Hutchinson, 1958)

Whitley, M. J., *Battleships of World War Two* (London, Arms & Armour Press, 1998)

Winklareth, Robert J., *The Bismarck Chase: New Light on a Famous Engagement* (London, Chatham Publishing, 1998)

Winklareth, Robert J., *The Battle of the Denmark Strait: A Critical Analysis of the Bismarck's Singular Triumph* (Oxford, Casemate Publishing, 2012)

Zetterling, Niklas and Tamelander, Michael, *Bismarck: The Final Days of Germany's Greatest Battleship* (Newbury, Casemate Publishing, 2009)

INDEX